DATE DUE

MAY 0 6 2008			

DEMCO

CRITICAL ANTHOLOGIES OF NONFICTION WRITING ™

CRITICAL PERSPECTIVES ON ISLAM AND THE WESTERN WORLD

Edited by
Jonathan Johansen

THE ROSEN PUBLISHING GROUP, INC.
NEW YORK

Published in 2006 by The Rosen Publishing Group, Inc.
29 East 21st Street, New York, NY 10010

Library of Congress Cataloging-in-Publication Data

Critical Perspectives on Islam and the Western World /[edited by]
Jonathan Johansen.
    p. cm.—Critical anthologies of nonfiction writing)
Includes bibliographical references and index.
ISBN 1-4042-0538-1 (library binding)
1. Islam—21st century. 2. Islam and world politics. 3. Terrorism—
Religious aspects—Islam. 4. Islamic fundamentalism. 5.
Islam—Relations.
I. Johansen, Jonathan. II. Series.
BP161.3.I728 2006
297.2'7—dc22
                                                            2005012621

Manufactured in the United States of America

On the cover: Hundreds of thousands of Muslims bow in prayer
toward the Kaaba on the streets of Mecca, 2001.

CONTENTS

INTRODUCTION

O f the world's major religions, Islam is the newest. It is younger than Hinduism, Buddhism, Judaism, and Christianity. The word "Islam" literally means "submission"—to the word and will of the religion's one god, Allah, as revealed to the prophet Muhammad and recorded in the religion's sacred text, the Koran (or Qur'an). Muslims, as the followers of Islam are known, believe that the Koran is the transcript of a tablet preserved in heaven that contains God's word and was revealed to his messenger, Muhammad, by the angel Gabriel over a period of twenty-three years. The revelations began as Muhammad was spending a night in solitary prayer and meditation in a cave on the Arabian Peninsula in about AD 610.

From its beginnings, Islam has presented itself as a challenge to the dominant religions of the West, Judaism and Christianity, both of which also have their origins in the Middle East. Islam teaches that both Judaism and Christianity possess divine truths, as revealed by God in the Bible. Christians and Jews are therefore regarded by Muslims as being, like themselves, "people of the book." Accordingly, Islam honors as wise and holy many of the revered figures of the Bible, such as Abraham, Moses, Joseph, Jonah, Noah, Job, kings David and Solomon, other prophets, John the Baptist, and even Mary, Jesus, and the apostles.

But Islam teaches that Jews and Christians have erred by straying from these divine revelations in many important ways, chiefly by dividing themselves into sects that disagree and quarrel about the meaning of biblical truths; by disobeying God's commandments; and by mistakenly regarding many figures as possessing divine attributes. "Allah is one and has no associates," Islam teaches. "There is no god but God" is another way of expressing the same concept, that only God is divine, and divinity cannot be divided or shared among his followers, prophets, saints, or messengers. Islam therefore regards as dangerously mistaken the idea that Jesus was God's son in human form; it teaches instead that Jesus is to be regarded as a great prophet but not divine. Similarly, it regards the Christian devotion to saints as a form of idolatry—worshipping something that is human as divine. Likewise, Muslims believe that the Jews were mistaken in rejecting Jesus's teachings, although not in rejecting his supposed divinity. Muslims believe that Islam, as revealed by Allah to Muhammad, the "last prophet," represents a return to the true religion; it had been previously divinely revealed to the Jewish patriarch Abraham, but then corrupted through human failings.

From its beginning then, Islam presented an implicit and express challenge to other religious and cultural traditions, particularly those of Europe (and later the Americas). Within little more than a century, Islam had spread widely in all four directions from the cities of Mecca and Medina (in present-day Saudi Arabia), winning adherents westward across the entire north of Africa above the Sahara and then upward into Europe through the Iberian Peninsula as far north as the Pyrenees; eastward across Persia (modern-day Iran) into India; southward along the entire eastern coast of Africa; and northward and eastward through Asia Minor into central Asia.

Religious, political, economic, and military conflict was inevitable; at stake were souls, cultural traditions, trade routes, and political power. The conflict culminated in the Crusades (1095–1291) of the Middle Ages, when the various Christian kingdoms of Europe sent armed forces to liberate the Holy Land from its various Islamic rulers.

Over the succeeding centuries, Islam continued to grow. Although it made some inroads in Europe, particularly on the Balkan Peninsula, it was driven from Spain. The new areas it influenced most were in Africa and to the east, particularly in India, China, and in the various islands eventually consolidated as the island nation of Indonesia. Under the political direction of the Ottoman Empire, it also consolidated its sway over the lands of the Middle East.

Today, Islam has more followers than any other religion in the world, more than one billion worldwide. A common perception in the West is that Islam is an "Arab" religion, but this is not quite accurate. Arabic is the language of Islam, but not all Arabs are Muslims, and not all Muslims are Arabs. The non-Arab nations of Indonesia, India, and Pakistan are the world's largest Muslim nations; and several non-Arab nations of central Asia, including Iran, Afghanistan, Kazakhstan, Uzbekistan, and Tajikistan, are important centers of Islam today.

In the twentieth century, the relationship of Islam and the Western world entered an important new phase in its history. At the end of World War I (1914–1918), the defeat and dismantling of the Ottoman Empire meant that the Arab lands of the Middle East, which had been under Ottoman rule for centuries, now came under new leadership. Many of these lands, such as Syria, Palestine, Jordan, Saudi Arabia, and Iraq, were ruled first as colonies of Britain and France before becoming independent. Several decades later, at the end of World War II (1939–1945), nations such as India, Pakistan, and Indonesia, which were also home to huge Muslim populations, were also gaining their independence.

At the same time that the Arab nations of the Middle East were achieving independence, they were also becoming the subject of intensified interest on the part of the richer, more powerful nations of the West, particularly the United States. The reason was the discovery that the territories of many of these new Arab nations contained the largest untapped reserves of the world's most important commodity—oil. In a continually modernizing, industrialized world, access to sufficient oil reserves is the single most important geopolitical strategic imperative for Western powers.

An immediate result was a heightened Western—especially American—presence and influence in many of these countries. Oil brought wealth and, above all, rapid change to these largely traditional societies. In some instances, the resulting change was criticized by Muslim members of these societies as not being rapid or extensive enough. For example, a nation's newfound wealth would not be distributed equally among members of society, or lead to increased cultural and political freedoms and democracy as found in the Western world. At the same time, others criticized the changes brought by wealth and Western influence, no matter how advanced or progressive they might seem, as destructive of the traditional values of their societies. Those threatened, traditional values were increasingly seen as Islamic values. Embracing these values came to be seen as one way that Muslim societies could preserve and protect their identities without being swallowed up by the richer, more materialistic, more permissive societies of the "nonbelievers" in the West.

For many Muslims, this threat is embodied most graphically by the creation of the State of Israel in the Middle East. Responding to decades of Zionism (the movement that began in the nineteenth century calling for the return of Jewish people to Palestine) and to the massacre of 6 million European Jews during World War II, the United Nations created a "Jewish homeland" in Palestine following World War II. Israel declared its independence as a nation in 1948. Many Arabs and Muslims viewed Israel's creation as coming at the expense of the Arab population of Palestine, known as Palestinians. That resentment increased as Israel, initially tiny, steadily occupied new territory after defeating its Arab neighbors in a series of wars, thereby displacing an ever-increasing number of Palestinians. The Israel-Palestinian question remains a flash point in relations between Islam and the Western world. The fact that Israel is dependent on U.S. economic and military aid for its survival leads some Muslims to equate the United States and Israel. The inability of the governments of Arab states to more effectively oppose Israel and obtain concrete gains for the Palestinians has served to reinforce the belief of some Muslims that their societies and leaders have been unable to resist Western—especially American—power and influence.

One consequence of these events has been the rise of so-called Islamist, or Islamic, fundamentalist movements throughout the Muslim world. Characteristic of such movements is the belief that Islam is not just a set of religious practices but an organized, coherent system of law, behavior, and government that can be used to organize an entire society. Such Islamist beliefs have inspired both revolution and resistance on a national scale, as in Iran and Afghanistan. Islamic groups such as the Palestine Liberation Organization (PLO), Hamas, Hezbollah, and Islamic Jihad, have initiated violent, terrorist activity against Western targets, culminating in the devastating attack by Al Qaeda against the United States on September 11, 2001. The September 11 attack, and the resulting war on terrorism, sponsored by the United States, have led many people in both the West and the Muslim world to ask whether the values, beliefs, and culture of the Western and Islamic worlds are so fundamentally opposed as to make violent conflict between Islam and the West inevitable in today's world. —*JJ*

CHAPTER ONE

TIME, CONTINUITY, AND CHANGE: ISLAMS'S VIEW OF THE WEST

Shaykh Muhammad ibn Abdul-Wahhab (1703–1792) was an eighteenth-century Muslim preacher on the Arabian Peninsula who believed Islam had been badly corrupted since the time of the prophet Muhammad. In particular, he objected to excessive veneration of Muhammad and other Muslim holy men, which he regarded as akin to the worship of Christian saints; veneration of tombs and other holy sites; and luxurious forms of worship and living. In response, he advocated a return to the most fundamental interpretation of the Koran and the elimination of all additions to Islam since the time of Muhammad. He also advocated a strict and literal interpretation of Islamic law, the sharia, with its prescription of public corporal punishment for various transgressions, (such as stoning for adultery and the amputation of hands for thievery).

The reform movement Abdul-Wahhab championed is sometimes referred to as Wahhabism, although its followers regard this designation as an insult. They prefer to be referred to as Salafis, which means "those who follow the ways of the forefathers." They believe that the concept known as Tawhid, which is sometimes defined as "faith in the unity of God," should serve as the basis for all individual action and even for the organization of society. (Muslims express the concept of Tawhid most simply and eloquently: "There is no god but Allah.") In the essay below, Abdul-Wahhab uses verses from the Koran to explain the basic concept of Tawhid.

Abdul-Wahhab gained his most powerful and important followers among the Sauds, who would become the ruling royal family of the new nation of Saudi Arabia in the early decades of the twentieth century. Today, Saudi Arabia remains a Salafi kingdom, and its great wealth allows it to fund Salafi education and missionary work throughout the Islamic world. Salafi principles have also inspired many different Islamist groups of recent years, especially those (such as Al Qaeda), who consider it their duty to carry out jihad, or holy war, against those they regard as the enemies of Islam. —JJ

"Four Basic Rules of Pure Monotheism"
by Shaykh Muhammad ibn Abdul-Wahhab
1736

Almighty God, Lord of the Glorious Throne, I pray that He may guide you in this world and the next; that He may always bless you; that He may make you one of those who recognize His bounty, who remain firm in face of adversity, and who repent and seek His forgiveness if they disobey or sin. These three characteristics are the indices of felicity and blessedness.

Know that pure worship and monotheism, which is the religion of Abraham, consists of worshipping God alone, of dedicating yourself sincerely to serving Him. God said:

"I have not created jinn and men but to worship Me."
[Qur'an 51:56]

Once you know that God has created you to serve Him, you will realize that there can be no service except with Pure Monotheism *(Arabic: Tawhid)*. Just as there is no formal prayer without purity, and there is no purity with uncleanliness, so there is no worship of God while worshipping others along with Him *(Arabic: Shirk)*. By associating others with Almighty God, man's worship is spoilt, his deeds are vain and he is doomed to eternal Hellfire. If you are cognizant of all this, you will realize that your most important care should be to have all the knowledge pertinent thereto, that God may save you from Hell's terrible abyss. Almighty God said:

God will not forgive any the association of anything with Him; but He will forgive any lesser offense to whomsoever He chooses. [Qur'an 4:47, 115]

It should be mentioned that Almighty God will forgive those who have ascribed partners Him, or worshipped others along with Him, if they repent from doing it before they die.

Such pertinent knowledge consists of four basic rules, elaborated in Almighty God's Holy Book.

First Rule:

The first rule is the knowledge that the unbelieving pagans whom the Prophet Muhammad, the peace and grace of God be upon him, opposed, did acknowledge that Almighty God—May He be glorified—is indeed the Creator, Provider and Maker of this world. However, this did not make them Muslims. Evidence therefore is in the verse:

> *Ask them: "Who sends down for you your provision from the sky and grows it out of the earth? Who hears your prayer and sees your condition? Who brings the living out of the dead and the dead out of the living? Who directs the course of the world?" They will answer: "God." Answer: "Would you then not fulfill your duty to Him?"* [Qur'an 10:32]

Second Rule:

The second rule is to know that the unbelievers claim that they do not pray to their objects of worship and call on them except to the end that they may intercede on their behalf with God, as the verse said:

> *Those who worshipped others as patrons beside God, claiming that they did so only to come through their intercession nearer to Him, will receive the judgment of God in the matter they contend. God will not guide the ingrate, the liar.* [Qur'an 39:3]

Evidence regarding intercession is in the verse:

They serve beside God beings which can neither benefit nor harm, claiming, "These are our intercessors with God."
[Qur'an 10:18]

There are two kinds of intercession, one illegitimate and the other legitimate. The former is that which is sought from sources other than God regarding matters where all the power lies in God alone. Evidence for this is in the verse:

O men who believe, spend of that which We have provided for you before the Day when there will be neither sale nor purchase, neither favors nor intercession. The unbelievers are themselves unjust. [Qur'an 2:254]

The legitimate intercession is that which is asked of Almighty God, where the intercessor receives his power from Him, and the interceded for is he whom God is pleased to accept as such for his word and deed. Almighty God said:

No one may intercede with God except by His permission.
[Qur'an 2:55].

Third Rule:

The third rule is the knowledge that the Prophet Muhammad, may God bless him and give him peace, appeared among people of many religious traditions. Some worshipped angels; others worshipped the prophets and saints of God; others worshipped trees and stones, sun and moon. All of these peoples were fought by him, as they must, relentlessly without distinction. Evidence therefore is in the following Qur'ânic verses:

And fight them, that there may be no aberration in religion, and all religion belongs to Almighty God. [Qur'an 2:193]

Day and night, sun and moon, are His creation and sign. Do not worship the sun or the moon, but God, their Creator, if you seek the truth. [Qur'an 41:37]

Almighty God does not command you to take the angels and prophets as Lords. [Qur'an 3:80]

And God said to Jesus, son of Mary: "Did you ask men to take you and your mother for objects of worship beside Almighty God?" He answered: "Praise be to You, O God! How can I have asked that which is not mine to ask? If I did, You know it and all that is in my mind. I do not know what is in Your mind, O Transcendent, All-Knowing God! I have not conveyed to them except what You have commanded me to convey, namely, Worship and serve God, my and your only Lord. I was a witness for You in their midst. When You caused me to die, You took over the witnessing on them as well as on all else. If You punish them, they are Your creatures; and if You forgive them, You are the Mighty, the Wise." [Qur'an 5:116–118]

Those unto whom they pray [i.e., the saints] *themselves seek an avenue to their Lord's mercy, compete in coming*

close to Almighty God, and fear His punishment.
Punishment of your Lord is certainly to be shunned.
[Qur'an 17:57]

Have you considered al-Lat, al-'Uzza and the third one
Manat? (The names of false gods which were worshipped by
the pre-Islamic Arabs) Are yours the males and His the
females? Is this not ridiculous? All of them are but names
which you have named, following the example of your
ancestors. God gave no voucher for them. You follow but a
guess and your own desires. [Qur'an 53:19–23]

Fourth Rule:

The people who associate partners with Almighty God, in
both belief and worship, in our own day are worse and hence
more guilty than those of pre-Islamic times. For, the ancient
ones used to only worship others besides God in prosperity
and return to genuine faith in adversity, whereas the present
day associationists are constant in their unbelief, regardless
of prosperity or adversity. Evidence for this is in the
Qur'ânic verse:

And when they ride in barks [in stormy seas]
they address their prayers to Almighty God in complete sin-
cerity, but relapse into shirk [i.e. associating partners
with Him] *when they reach the shore.* [Qur'an 29:65]

May the peace and blessings of Almighty God be upon
Muhammad, his Companions and all those who follow him
until the Last Day.

Inspired by Salafi teachings, the schoolteacher Hassan al-Banna (1906–1949) founded the Muslim Brotherhood in his native Egypt in 1928. The group was initially devoted to driving the British rulers of Egypt from the country. In later decades, once Egypt gained true self-rule, the Brotherhood was equally devoted to opposing, violently at times, the Egyptian government. It regarded the Egyptian government as insufficiently dedicated to Islamist principles and too beholden to Western powers—initially the Soviet Union and then, especially, the United States and Israel. The group also won supporters by providing social services, such as education and medical care, to the poorer members of Egyptian society and by its early and consistent support for the Palestinian cause. Though al-Banna was assassinated in 1949, probably by Egyptian security forces, the Muslim Brotherhood has remained a prominent force in Egyptian society and throughout the Muslim world. It has also inspired numerous similar organizations.

In this selection from "Between Yesterday and Today," one of al-Banna's essays from the 1930s, he decries the West for the materialistic, spiritually empty way of life it has introduced to Egypt and other Muslim societies and proposes organized resistance based on Islamic principles. —JJ

From "Between Yesterday and Today"
by Hassan al-Banna
1936

The Europeans worked assiduously in trying to immerse (the world) in materialism, with their corrupting traits and murderous germs, to overwhelm those Muslim lands that their hands stretched out to. Under their authority the Muslims suffered an ill fate, for while they secured for themselves power and prosperity through science, knowledge, industry, and good organisation, the Muslims were barred from all this. They laid the plans for this social turmoil in masterly fashion, invoking the aid of their political intellect and military might until they achieved their goal. They deluded the Muslim leaders by granting them loans and entering into financial transactions with them—An easy task which enabled them to infiltrate the economy and flood the country with their capital, their banks, and their companies; Thus they ran the economic machinery, exploiting the enormous profits and vast sums of money. All to the exclusion of the inhabitants. Hence, they were able to alter the basic principles of government, justice, and education, and infuse in the most powerful Islamic countries, their own peculiar political judicial, and cultural systems. They imported their semi-naked women into these regions, together with their liquors, their theatres, their dance halls, their amusements arcades, their stories, their newspapers, their novels, their whims, their silly games, and their vices. Here they allowed for crimes intolerable in their own countries, and beautified this tumultuous world to the deluded, naive eyes of wealthy Muslims and those of rank and authority. This was not enough for them, so they built schools and scientific cultural institutes, casting doubt and heresy within the hearts of people. They taught them how to demean themselves, to vilify their religion and their homeland, to detach themselves from their beliefs, and to regard anything Western as sacred, in the belief that only that which is European can be emulated. These schools were restricted to the upper class, the ruling body, the powerful and the future leaders. Those who were unsuccessful in such places were sent abroad to complete their studies. This drastic, well organised social campaign was tremendously successful since it appealed to the mind. It will continue to exert its strong intellectual influence over a long period of time. Thus, it was far more dangerous than any political or military campaign. Some Islamic countries went overboard in their admiration for the European civilisation and their dissatisfaction with the Islamic one, to the point that Turkey declared itself a non-Islamic state, imitating the Europeans in everything that they did. Aman Allah Khan, King of Afghanistan, tried this, but the attempt lost him his throne. In Egypt the manifestations of this mimicry increased and became so serious that one of the intellectual leaders could openly say that the only path to progress was to adopt this civilisation: good or evil, bitter or sweet, praise worthy or reprehensible. From Egypt it spread with strength and speed into the neighbouring countries, to the extent that it reached Morocco and encircled the holy sanctuaries within the midst of Hijaz . . .

Awakening: Just as political aggression had its effect in arousing nationalist feelings, so has social aggression in reviving the Islamic ideology. Voices have been raised in every land, demanding a return to Islam, an understanding of its precepts, and an application of its rules. The day must soon come when the walls of this materialistic civilisation will come down upon the heads of its inhabitants. Then their hearts and souls will burn with a spiritual hunger, but they will find no sustenance, no healing, no remedy, except in the teachings of this Noble Book . . .

What do we want, dear brothers? Do we seek temporary goals such as hoarding up wealth and becoming famous? Or do we want dominion over the earth? . . .

May Allah witness that we do not want any of these, that our work and our mission are not toward these ends. Rather always bear in mind that you have two fundamental goals:

1) Freeing the Islamic homeland from all foreign authority, for this is a natural right belonging to every human being which only the unjust oppressor will deny.
2) The establishment of an Islamic state within this homeland, which acts according to the precepts of Islam, applies its social regulations, advocates its sound principles, and broadcasts its mission to all of mankind.

For as long as this state does not emerge, every Muslim is sinning and is responsible before Allah the Almighty for the failure and slackness in establishing it. In these bewildering circumstances, it is against the interests of humanity that a state advocating injustice and oppression should arise, while there should be no one at all working for the advent of a state founded on truth, justice, and peace. We want to accomplish

these two goals in the Nile Valley and the Arab kingdom, and
in every land which Allah has blessed with the Islamic creed:
uniting all the Muslims . . .

Apart from these two aims, we have some specific aims,
If they are not accomplished our society cannot become
wholly Islamic. Dear brothers, recall that more than sixty
percent of the Egyptians live at a subhuman level. Only
through the most arduous toil do they get enough to eat.
Egypt is threatened by murderous famines and exposed to
many economic problems, the outcome of which only Allah
can know. Recall too that there are more than 320 foreign
companies in Egypt, monopolising all the public utilities and
important facilities in every sector of the country; the wheels
of commerce, industry, and all economic institutions are in
the hands of profiteering foreigners; our wealth in land is
being transferred with lightning speed from our hands to
those of others. Recall also that, out of the entire civilised
world, Egypt is subject to the most diseases, plagues, and illness; over 90 percent of the Egyptian people are threatened
by physical infirmity, the loss of some sensory perception,
and a variety of sicknesses and ailments; Egypt is still back-
ward, with no more than one fifth of the population
possessing any form of education, and of these more than
one hundred thousand have never gone further than the primary school level. Recall that crime has doubled in Egypt,
and that it is increasing at an alarming rate to the point that
there are more people coming out of prisons than schools;
that up to the present time Egypt has been unable to properly outfit a single army division; These symptoms and
phenomena may be observed in any Islamic country. Amid

your aims are to work in reforming education; to fight poverty, ignorance, disease, and crime; and to create an exemplary society deserving to be associated with the Islamic Sharee'ah . . .

How will we arrive at these goals? Speeches, announcements, letters, lessons, lectures, a diagnosis of the ailment and a prescription of the medicine. All these by themselves are useless and will never achieve, nor help achieve a single aim. Nevertheless, every mission has an approach which it must adopt and act accordingly. It remains invariable and unchanging, and is confined to the following three matters:

1) Deep faith
2) Precise organization
3) Uninterrupted work

This is our general approach dear brothers, so have conviction in your ideology, rally around it and work steadfastly for it . . .

Besides this general approach, there may be further measures that have to be adopted and strictly adhered to. They may have both positive and negative aspects to them, either in compatibility with man's customary habits or in stark contradiction. Some are mild while others are rigorous, so we must train ourselves and prepare to face all this in order to guarantee success. We may be asked to break old customs and habits, to conform to unfamiliar backgrounds and settings. For in reality our mission is to change that which is prevailing and conventional. Are you prepared for this, dear brothers? . . .

Many people will say: What do these measures mean? How can they build a nation or maintain a society burdened with such chronic problems and sunk in a welter of corruption? How will you manage the economy on a non profit basis? How will you respond to the woman question? How will you obtain your rights without the use of force?

Dear brothers, know that Satan slips his devilish bid into the aspirations of every reformer, but Allah cancels out what Satan whispers; then Allah decrees His miracles, for Allah is Knowing, Wise. Remind these people that history teaches us lessons about past and contemporary nations; any nation determined to live cannot possibly die.

The Egyptian novelist, poet, philosopher, and scholar Sayyid al-Qutb (1906–1966) is the most important intellectual influence on today's Islamist groups, especially such violent, terrorist offshoots as Al Qaeda. American scholar Paul Berman has called al-Qutb "the philosopher of Islamic terror" and notes that he is "the intellectual hero of every one of the groups that eventually went into Al-Qaeda."

Al-Qutb memorized the entire Koran by the age of ten, received a secular education at the University of Cairo, and even obtained a master's degree in education in the United States in the 1940s at Colorado State Teachers College (now called the University of Northern Colorado). He was appalled by what he regarded as the decadence, permissiveness, corruption, and materialism of American society. When he returned to Egypt, he joined the Muslim Brotherhood, succeeding al-Banna as its most important voice, and becoming the significant intellectual exponent of Islamism in the Muslim world, He called for jihad, or holy war, to create new societies based on the principles of the Koran.

The Egyptian government began to move against the Muslim Brotherhood, and al-Qutb was imprisoned in 1954. He spent most of the rest of his life in prison before being executed in 1966. The selection here is the famous introduction from his best-known book, Milestones, *which he wrote while in prison. In it, al-Qutb asserts that what was occurring in the world, even within the Arab nations, at the instigation of the West was nothing less than "a final offensive . . . to extermi-nate [Islam] as even a basic creed and to replace it with secular conceptions having their own implications, val-ues, institutions, and organizations." He speaks of the world as entering a new period of* Jahiliyya—*the period of darkness, ignorance, and superstition that prevailed before Allah's revelations to Muhammad. —JJ*

From *Milestones*
by Sayyid al-Qutb
1964

Mankind today is on the brink of a precipice, not because of the danger of complete annihilation which is hanging over its head—this being just a symptom and not the real disease—but because humanity is devoid of those vital values which are necessary not only for its healthy development but also for its real progress. Even the Western world realizes that Western civilization is unable to present any healthy values for the guidance of mankind. It knows that it does not possess anything which will satisfy its own conscience and justify its existence.

Democracy in the West has become infertile to such an extent that it is borrowing from the systems of the Eastern bloc, especially in the economic system, under the name of socialism. It is the same with the Eastern bloc. Its social theories, foremost among which is Marxism, in the beginning attracted not only a large number of people from the East but also from the West, as it was a way of life based on a creed. But now Marxism is defeated on the plane of thought, and if it is stated that not a single nation in the world is truly Marxist, it will not be an exaggeration. On the whole this theory conflicts with man's nature and its needs. This ideology prospers only in a degenerate society or in a society which has become cowed as a result of some form of prolonged dictatorship. But now, even under these circumstances, its materialistic economic system is failing, although this was the only foundation on which its structure was based. Russia, which is the leader of the communist countries, is itself suffering from shortages of food. Although during the times of the Tsars Russia used to produce surplus food, it now has to import food from abroad and has to sell its reserves of gold for this purpose. The main reason for this is the failure of the system of collective farming, or, one can say, the failure of a system which is against human nature.

It is essential for mankind to have new leadership!

The leadership of mankind by Western man is now on the decline, not because Western culture has become poor materially or because its economic and military power has become weak. The period of the Western system has come to an end primarily because it is deprived of those life-giving values which enabled it to be the leader of mankind.

It is necessary for the new leadership to preserve and develop the material fruits of the creative genius of Europe, and also to provide mankind with such high ideals and values as have so far remained undiscovered by mankind, and which will also acquaint humanity with a way of life which is harmonious with human nature, which is positive and constructive, and which is practicable.

Islam is the only System which possesses these values and this way of life.

The period of the resurgence of science has also come to an end. This period, which began with the Renaissance in the sixteenth century after Christ and reached its zenith in the eighteenth and nineteenth centuries, does not possess a reviving spirit.

All nationalistic and chauvinistic ideologies which have appeared in modern times, and all the movements and theories derived from them, have also lost their vitality. In short, all man-made individual or collective theories have proved to be failures.

At this crucial and bewildering juncture, the turn of Islam and the Muslim community has arrived—the turn of Islam, which does not prohibit material inventions. Indeed, it counts it as an obligation on man from the very beginning of time, when God deputed him as His representative on earth, and regards it under certain conditions as worship of God and one of the purposes of man's creation.

And when Your Sustainer said to the angels, I am going to make My representative on earth. (Qur'an 2:30)

And I have not created jinns and men except that they worship Me. (2:143)

Thus the turn of the Muslim community has come to fulfill the task for mankind which God has enjoined upon it.

You are the best community raised for the good of mankind. You enjoin what is good and forbid what is wrong, and you believe in God. (3:110)

Thus We have made you a middle community, so that you be witnesses for mankind as the Messenger is a witness for you. (2:143)

Islam cannot fulfill its role except by taking concrete form in a society, rather, in a nation; for man does not listen, especially in this age, to an abstract theory which is not seen materialized in a living society. From this point of view, we can say that the Muslim community has been extinct for a few centuries, for this Muslim community does not denote the name of a land in which Islam resides, nor is it a people whose forefathers lived under the Islamic system at some earlier time. It is the name of a group of people whose manners, ideas and concepts, rules and regulations, values and criteria, are all derived from the Islamic source. The Muslim community with these characteristics vanished at the moment the laws of God became suspended on earth.

If Islam is again to play the role of the leader of mankind, then it is necessary that the Muslim community be restored to its original form.

It is necessary to revive that Muslim community which is buried under the debris of the man-made traditions of several generations, and which is crushed under the weight of those false laws and customs which are not even remotely related to the Islamic teachings, and which, in spite of all this, calls itself the "world of Islam."

I am aware that between the attempt at "revival" and the attainment of "leadership" there is a great distance, as the Muslim community has long ago vanished from existence and from observation, and the leadership of mankind has long since passed to other ideologies and other nations, other concepts and other systems. This was the era during which Europe's genius created its marvelous works in science, culture, law and material production, due to which mankind has progressed to great heights of creativity and material comfort. It is not easy to find fault with the inventors of such marvelous things, especially since what we call the "world of Islam" is completely devoid of all this beauty.

But in spite of all this, it is necessary to revive Islam. The distance between the revival of Islam and the attainment of world leadership may be vast, and there may be great difficulties on the way; but the first step must be taken for the revival of Islam.

If we are to perform our task with insight and wisdom, we must first know clearly the nature of those qualities on the basis of which the Muslim community can fulfill its obligation as the leader of the world. This is essential so that we may not commit any blunders at the very first stage of its reconstruction and revival.

The Muslim community today is neither capable of nor required to present before mankind great genius in material inventions, which will make the world bow its head before its supremacy and thus re-establish once more its world leadership. Europe's creative mind is far ahead in this area, and at least for a few centuries to come we cannot expect to compete with Europe and attain supremacy over it in these fields.

Hence we must have some other quality, that quality which modern civilization does not possess.

But this does not mean that we should neglect material progress. We should also give our full attention and effort in this direction, not because at this stage it is an essential requirement for attaining the leadership of mankind, but because it is an essential condition for our very existence; and Islam itself, which elevates man to the position of representative of God on earth, and which, under certain conditions, considers the responsibilities of this representative as the worship of God and the purpose of man's creation, makes material progress obligatory for us.

To attain the leadership of mankind, we must have something to offer besides material progress, and this other quality can only be a faith and a way of life which on the one hand conserves the benefits of modern science and technology, and on the other fulfills the basic human needs on the same level of excellence as technology has fulfilled them in the sphere of material comfort. And then this faith and way of life must take concrete form in a human society—in other words, In a Muslim society.

If we look at the sources and foundations of modern ways of living, it becomes clear that the whole world is steeped in Jahiliyyah [Ignorance of the Divine guidance] and all the marvelous material comforts and high-level inventions do not diminish this ignorance. This Jahiliyyah is based on rebellion against God's sovereignty on earth. It transfers to man one of the greatest attributes of God, namely sovereignty, and makes some men lords over others. It is now not in that simple and primitive form of the ancient Jahiliyyah, but takes the form of claiming that the right to create values, to legislate rules of collective behavior, and to choose any way of life rests with men, without regard to what God has prescribed. The result of this rebellion against the authority of God is the oppression of His creatures. Thus the humiliation of the common man under the communist systems and the exploitation of individuals and nations due to greed for wealth and imperialism under the capitalist systems are but a corollary of rebellion against God's authority and the denial of the dignity of man given to him by God.

In this respect, Islam's way of life is unique, for in systems other than Islam, some people worship others in some form or another. Only in the Islamic way of life do all men become free from the servitude of some men to others and devote themselves to the worship of God alone, deriving guidance from Him alone, and bowing before Him alone.

This is where the roads separate, and this is that new concept which we possess and can present to mankind—this and the way of life which this concept organizes for all the practical aspects of man's life. This is that vital message of which mankind does not know. It is not a product of Western invention nor of European genius, whether eastern or western.

Without doubt, we possess this new thing which is perfect to the highest degree, a thing which mankind does not know about and is not capable of "producing."

But as we have stated before, the beauty of this new system cannot be appreciated unless it takes a concrete form. Hence it is essential that a community arrange its affairs according to it and show it to the world. In order to bring this about, we need to initiate the movement of Islamic revival in some Muslim country. Only such a revivalist movement will eventually attain to the status of world leadership, whether the distance is near or far. How is it possible to start the task of reviving Islam?

It is necessary that there should be a vanguard which sets out with this determination and then keeps walking on the path, marching through the vast ocean of Jahiliyyah which has encompassed the entire world. During its course, it should keep itself somewhat aloof from this all-encompassing Jahiliyyah and should also keep some ties with it.

It is necessary that this vanguard should know the landmarks and the milestones of the road toward this goal so that they may recognize the starting place, the nature, the responsibilities and the ultimate purpose of this long journey. Not only this, but they ought to be aware of their position as opposed to this Jahiliyyah, which has struck its stakes throughout the earth: when to co-operate with others and when to separate from them: what characteristics and qualities they should cultivate, and with what characteristics and qualities the Jahiliyyah immediately surrounding them is armed; how to address the people of Jahiliyyah in the language of Islam, and what topics and problems ought to be discussed; and where and how to obtain guidance in all these matters.

The milestones will necessarily be determined by the light of the first source of this faith—the Holy Qur'an—and from its basic teachings, and from the concept which it created in the minds of the first group of Muslims, those whom God raised to fulfill His will, those who once changed the course of human history in the direction ordained by God.

I have written "Milestones" for this vanguard, which I consider to be a waiting reality about to be materialized. Four chapters [These chapters are "The Nature of the Qur'anic Method," "Islamic Concept and Culture," "Jihaad in the Cause of God," and "Revival of the Muslim Community and its characteristics."] are taken from my commentary, *Fi Jilal al-Qur'an*, [*In the Shade of the Qur'an*, a commentary on the Qur'an] which I have changed here and there slightly to suit the topic. This introduction and the other chapters I wrote at various times. In writing these chapters I have set down the deep truths which I grasped during my meditations over the way of life presented in the Holy Qur'an. These thoughts may appear random and disconnected, but one thing is common among them; that is, these thoughts are milestones on the road, and it is the nature of signs along the road to be disconnected. Taken together, these writings are a first installment of a series, and with God's help I hope to write some more collections on this topic.

And the guidance is from God.

*Along with al-Qutb, Sayyi Abul Ala Maududi
(1903–1979) is one of the most important intellectual
figures of the modern Islamist movements. Maududi was
born in India and later became a citizen of Pakistan. His
influence has been greatest in the more eastern regions of
the Muslim world, particularly in India, Pakistan,
Afghanistan, and the former Soviet republics of central
Asia. Like al-Qutb, Maududi advocated "Islamic jihad to
eliminate the rule of a non-Islamic system and establish
instead an Islamic system of state rule." According to
Maududi, "Islam does not intend to confine this revolution to a single State or a few countries; the aim of
Islam is to bring about a universal revolution."*

*Maududi was an extremely prolific author who
wrote more than 100 books and countless pamphlets and
manifestos. The selection below is an excerpt from his
book* Towards Understanding Islam*. In it, he explains
how an embrace of the Islamic concept of Tawhid can
serve as the basis for a true and complete understanding
of the entire world in all its mystifying complexities and
manifestations. —JJ*

From *Towards Understanding Islam*
by Sayyid Abul Ala Maududi
1960

From the earliest known history of man as well as from the
oldest relics of antiquity that we have been able to obtain, it

appears that in every age man recognised some deity or deities and worshipped them. Even today every nation, from the most primitive to the most advanced, believes in and worships some deity. Having a deity and worshipping him is ingrained in human nature. There is something within man's soul which forces him to do so.

But the question is: what is that thing and why does man feel impelled to do so? The answer to this question can be discovered if we look at the position of man in this huge universe. Neither man nor his nature is omnipotent. He is neither self-sufficient nor self-existing; nor are his powers limitless. In fact, he is weak, frail, needy and destitute.

He is dependent on a multitude of forces to maintain his existence, but all of them are not essentially and totally within his powers. Sometimes they come into his possession in a simple and natural way, and at times he finds himself deprived of them. There are many important and valuable things which he endeavours to get, but sometimes he succeeds in getting them, while sometimes he does not, for it is not completely in his own power to obtain them. There are many things injurious to him; accidents destroy his life's work in a single moment; chance brings his hopes to a sudden end; illness, worries and calamities are always threatening him and marring his way to happiness. He attempts to get rid of them, and meets with both success and failure.

There are many things whose greatness and grandeur overawe him: mountains and rivers, gigantic animals and ferocious beasts. He experiences earthquakes, storms and other natural disasters. He observes clouds over his head and sees them becoming thick and dark, with peals of thunder, flashes of lightning and heavy rain. He sees the sun, the moon and the stars in their constant motions. He reflects how great, powerful and grand these bodies are, and, in contrast to them, how frail and insignificant he himself is!

These vast phenomena, on the one hand, and the consciousness of his own frailty, on the other, impress him with a deep sense of his own weakness, humbleness and helplessness. And it is quite natural that a primitive idea of divinity should coincide with this sense. He thinks of the hands which are wielding these great forces. The sense of their greatness makes him bow in humility. The sense of their powerfulness makes him seek their help. He tries to please them so that they may be beneficial to him, and he fears them and tries to escape their wrath so that he may not be destroyed by them.

In the most primitive stage of ignorance, man thinks that the great objects of nature whose grandeur and glory are visible, and which appear to be injurious or beneficial to him, hold in themselves the real power and authority, and, therefore, are divine. Thus he worships trees, animals, rivers, mountains, fire, rain, air, heavenly bodies and numerous other objects. This is the worst form of ignorance.

When his ignorance dissipates to some extent and some glimmers of light and knowledge appear on his intellectual horizon, he comes to know that these great and powerful objects are in themselves as helpless and dependent, or rather, they are still more dependent and helpless. The biggest and the strongest animal dies like a tiny germ, and loses all his power; great rivers rise and fall and become dry; the highest mountains are blasted and shattered by man himself; the productiveness of the earth is not under the earth's control—water makes it

prosperous and lack of water makes it barren. Even water is
not independent. It depends on air which brings the clouds.
Air, too, is powerless and its usefulness depends on other
causes. The moon, the sun, and the stars are also bound by
a powerful law outside whose dictates they cannot make the
slightest movement.

After these considerations man's mind turns to the possibility of some great mysterious power of divine nature which
controls the objects he sees and which may be the repository
of all authority. These reflections give rise to belief in mysterious powers behind natural phenomena, with innumerable gods
governing various parts and aspects of nature such as air, light
and water. Material forms or symbols are constructed to repre-
sent them and man begins to worship these forms and
symbols. This, too, is a form of ignorance, and reality remains
hidden to the human eye even at this stage of man's intellectual and cultural pilgrimage.

As man progresses still further in knowledge and learning, and as he reflects more and more deeply on the
fundamental problems of existence, he finds an all-powerful
law and all-encompassing control in the universe. What a
complete regularity is observed in sunrise and sunset, in
winds and rains, in the motions of stars and the changes of
seasons! With what a wonderful harmony countless different
forces are working jointly. And what a highly effective and
supremely wise law it is according to which all the various
causes in the universe are made to work together at an
appointed time to produce an appointed event! Observing this
uniformity, regularity and complete obedience to one great
law in all fields of Nature, even a polytheist finds himself

obliged to believe that there must be a deity greater than all the others, exercising supreme authority. For, if there were separate, independent deities, the whole machinery of the universe would be upset.

He calls this greatest deity by different names, such as Allah, Permeshwar, God, Khuda-i-Khuda'igan. But as the darkness of ignorance still persists, he continues worshipping minor deities along with the Supreme One. He imagines that the Divine Kingdom of God may not be different from earthly kingdoms. Just as a ruler has many ministers, trusted associates, governors and other responsible officers, so the minor deities are like so many responsible officers under the Great God Who cannot be approached without winning the favour of the officers under Him. So they must also be worshipped and appealed to for help, and should in no case be offended. They are taken as agents through whom an approach can be made to the Great God.

The more a man increases his knowledge, the greater becomes his dissatisfaction with the multiplicity of deities. So the number of minor deities begins to decrease. More enlightened men bring each one of them under the searchlight of scrutiny and ultimately find that none of these man-made deities has any divine character; they themselves are creatures like man, though rather more helpless. They are thus eliminated one by one until only one God remains.

But the concept of one God still contains some remnants of the elements of ignorance. Some people imagine that He has a body as men have, and is in a particular place. Some believe that God came down to earth in human form; others think that God, after settling the affairs of the universe, retired and is now resting. Some believe that it is necessary to approach God through the media of saints and spirits, and that nothing can be achieved without their intercession. Some imagine God to have a certain form or image, and they believe it necessary to keep that image before them for the purposes of worship.

Such distorted notions of godhead have persisted and lingered, and many of them are prevalent among different people even today . . .

Let us see what significant realities the concept of Tawhid—this little phrase: la ilaha illallah—embraces: what truth it conveys and what beliefs it fosters.

First, we are faced with the question of the universe. We are face to face with a grand, limitless universe. Man's mind cannot discern its beginning or visualise its end. It has been moving along its chartered course from time immemorial and is continuing its journey in the vast vista of the future. Creatures beyond number have appeared in it—and go on appearing every day. It is so bewildering that a thinking mind finds itself wonderstruck. Man is unable to understand and grasp its reality by his unaided vision. He cannot believe that all this has appeared just by chance or accident. The universe is not a fortuitous mass of matter. It is not a jumble of unco-ordinated objects. It is not a conglomeration of chaotic and meaningless things. All this cannot be without a Creator, a Designer, a Controller, a Governor.

But who can create and control this majestic universe? Only He can do so Who is Master of all; Who is Infinite and Eternal; Who is All-Powerful, All-Wise, Omnipotent and Omniscient; Who is All-Knowing and All-Seeing. He must have supreme authority over all that exists in the universe. He must possess limitless powers, must be Lord of the universe and all that it contains, must be free from every flaw and weakness and none may have the power to interfere with His work. Only such a Being can be the Creator, the Controller and the Governor of the universe.

Second, it is essential that all these divine attributes and powers must be vested in One Being: it is impossible for two or more personalities having equal powers and attributes to co-exist. They are bound to collide. Therefore, there must be one and only one Supreme Being having control over all others. You cannot think of two governors for the same province or two supreme commanders of the army! Similarly, the distribution of these powers among different deities, so that, for instance, one of them is all—knowledge, the other all—providence and still another life-giver—and each having an independent domain—is also unthinkable. The universe is an indivisible whole and each one of such deities will be dependent upon others in the execution of his task. Lack of co-ordination is bound to occur. And if this happened, the world would fall to pieces. These attributes are also untransferable. It is not possible that a certain attribute might be present in a certain deity at one time and at another time be found in another deity. A divine being who is incapable of remaining alive himself cannot give life to others. The one who cannot protect his own divine power cannot be suited to govern the vast limitless universe.

The more you reflect on the problem, the firmer must your conviction be that all these divine powers and attributes must exist in one and the same Being alone. Thus, polytheism is a form of ignorance that cannot stand rational scrutiny. It is a practical impossibility. The facts of life and nature do not fit in with it. They automatically bring men to Reality, that is Tawhid, the Unity of God.

Now, keeping in mind this concept of God, look closely at this vast universe. Exert yourself to the utmost and say if you find among all the objects that you see, among all the things that you perceive, among all that you can think, feel or imagine—all that your knowledge can comprehend—anyone possessing these attributes. The sun, the moon, the stars, animals, birds or fishes, matter, money, any man or a group of men—does any of them possess these attributes? Most certainly not! For everything in the universe is created, controlled and regulated, is dependent on others, is mortal and transitory; its slightest movements are controlled by an inexorable law from which there can be no deviation. Their helpless condition proves that the attire of divinity cannot fit their body. They do not possess the slightest trace of divinity and have absolutely nothing to do with it. It is a travesty of truth and a folly of the highest magnitude to attribute divine status to them . . .

But this is not the end of our quest. We have found that divinity is not vested in any material or human element of the universe, and that none of them possesses even the slightest trace of it. This leads us to the conclusion that there is a Supreme Being, over and above all that our eyes see in the universe, Who possesses Divine attributes, Who is the Will behind all phenomena, the Creator of this grand universe, the Controller of its superb Law, the Governor of its serene rhythm, the Administrator of all its workings: He is Allah, the Lord of the Universe and no one and nothing is associated in His Divinity. This is what illallah (but Allah) means.

This knowledge is superior to all other kinds of knowledge and the greater you exert yourself, the deeper will be your conviction that this is the starting-point of all knowledge. In every field of inquiry—be it that of physics, chemistry, astronomy, geology, biology, zoology, economics, politics, sociology or the humanities, you will find that the deeper you probe, the clearer become the indications of the truth of La ilaha illallah [there is no god but Allah]. It is this concept which opens up the doors of inquiry and investigation and illumines the pathways of knowledge with the light of reality. And if you deny or disregard this reality, you will find that at every step you meet disillusionment, for the denial of this primary truth robs everything in the universe of its meaning and significance.

CHAPTER TWO

INDIVIDUALS, GROUPS, AND INSTITUTIONS: THE WEST'S VIEW OF ISLAM

The September 11 attack on the United States by the Islamist terrorist group Al Qaeda shocked Americans in many ways. Accustomed to thinking of the United States as a benign, well-intentioned presence in the world, many Americans genuinely had a hard time understanding the basis for the enmity underlying the attacks. "Why do they hate us?" was a question asked by many Americans, apparently in genuine bewilderment.

The selections in this chapter attempt to examine, from a Western point of view, the reasons for the growing conflict between Islam and the West. Even well before the September 11 attacks, writers, scholars, and foreign policy experts were debating whether the divides between Islam and the West were based on economics and foreign policy, or on more deep-rooted, perhaps irreconcilable, religious and cultural differences.

In the United States, all such analyses generally begin with Bernard Lewis's 1990 seminal and controversial article "The Roots of Muslim Rage." A longtime professor at Princeton University, Lewis is widely considered one of the English-speaking world's foremost experts on Islam and the Arab world. —JJ

"The Roots of Muslim Rage"
by Bernard Lewis
Atlantic Monthly, **September 1990**

In one of his letters Thomas Jefferson remarked that in matters of religion "the maxim of civil government" should be reversed and we should rather say, "Divided we stand, united, we fall." In this remark Jefferson was setting forth with classic terseness an idea that has come to be regarded as essentially American: the separation of Church and State. This idea was not entirely new; it had some precedents in the writings of Spinoza, Locke, and the philosophers of the European Enlightenment. It was in the United States, however, that the principle was first given the force of law and gradually, in the course of two centuries, became a reality.

If the idea that religion and politics should be separated is relatively new, dating back a mere three hundred years, the idea that they are distinct dates back almost to the beginnings of Christianity. Christians are enjoined in their Scriptures to "render . . . unto Caesar the things which are Caesar's and unto God the things which are God's." While opinions have differed as to the real meaning of this phrase, it has generally been interpreted as legitimizing a situation in which two institutions exist side by side, each with its own laws and chain of authority—one concerned with religion, called the Church, the other concerned with politics, called the State. And since they are two, they may be joined or separated, subordinate or independent, and conflicts may arise between them over questions of demarcation and jurisdiction.

This formulation of the problems posed by the relations between religion and politics, and the possible solutions to those problems, arise from Christian, not universal, principles and experience. There are other religious traditions in which religion and politics are differently perceived, and in which, therefore, the problems and the possible solutions are radically different from those we know in the West. Most of these traditions, despite their often very high level of sophistication and achievement, remained or became local—limited to one region or one culture or one people. There is one, however, that in its worldwide distribution, its continuing vitality, its universalist aspirations, can be compared to Christianity, and that is Islam.

Islam is one of the world's great religions. Let me be explicit about what I, as a historian of Islam who is not a Muslim, mean by that. Islam has brought comfort and peace of mind to countless millions of men and women. It has given dignity and meaning to drab and impoverished lives. It has taught people of different races to live in brotherhood and people of different creeds to live side by side in reasonable tolerance. It inspired a great civilization in which others besides Muslims lived creative and useful lives and which, by its achievement, enriched the whole world. But Islam, like other religions, has also known periods when it inspired in some of its followers a mood of hatred and violence. It is our misfortune that part, though by no means all or even most, of the Muslim world is now going through such a period, and that much, though again not all, of that hatred is directed against us.

We should not exaggerate the dimensions of the problem. The Muslim world is far from unanimous in its rejection of the West, nor have the Muslim regions of the Third World been the most passionate and the most extreme in their hostility. There are still significant numbers, in some quarters perhaps a majority, of Muslims with whom we share certain basic cultural and moral, social and political, beliefs and aspirations; there is still an imposing Western presence—cultural, economic, diplomatic—in Muslim lands, some of which are Western allies. Certainly nowhere in the Muslim world, in the Middle East or elsewhere, has American policy suffered disasters or encountered problems comparable to those in Southeast Asia or Central America. There is no Cuba, no Vietnam, in the Muslim world, and no place where American forces are involved as combatants or even as "advisers." But there is a Libya, an Iran, and a Lebanon, and a surge of hatred that distresses, alarms, and above all baffles Americans.

At times this hatred goes beyond hostility to specific interests or actions or policies or even countries and becomes a rejection of Western civilization as such, not only what it does but what it is, and the principles and values that it practices and professes. These are indeed seen as innately evil, and those who promote or accept them as the "enemies of God."

This phrase, which recurs so frequently in the language of the Iranian leadership, in both their judicial proceedings and their political pronouncements, must seem very strange to the modern outsider, whether religious or secular. The idea that God has enemies, and needs human help in order to identify and dispose of them, is a little difficult to assimilate. It is not, however, all that alien. The concept of the enemies of God is familiar in preclassical and classical antiquity, and in both the Old and New Testaments, as well as in the Koran. A particularly relevant version of the idea occurs in the dualist religions of ancient Iran, whose cosmogony assumed not one but two supreme powers. The Zoroastrian devil, unlike the Christian or Muslim or Jewish devil, is not one of God's creatures performing some of God's more mysterious tasks but an independent power, a supreme force of evil engaged in a cosmic struggle against God. This belief influenced a number of Christian, Muslim, and Jewish sects, through Manichaeism and other routes. The almost forgotten religion of the Manichees has given its name to the perception of problems as a stark and simple conflict between matching forces of pure good and pure evil.

The Koran is of course strictly monotheistic, and recognizes one God, one universal power only. There is a struggle in human hearts between good and evil, between God's commandments and the tempter, but this is seen as a struggle ordained by God, with its outcome preordained by God, serving as a test of mankind, and not, as in some of the old dualist religions, a struggle in which mankind has a crucial part to play in bringing about the victory of good over evil. Despite this monotheism, Islam, like Judaism and Christianity, was at various stages influenced, especially in Iran, by the dualist idea of a cosmic clash of good and evil, light and darkness, order and chaos, truth and falsehood, God and the Adversary, variously known as devil, Iblis, Satan, and by other names.

The Rise of the House of Unbelief

In Islam the struggle of good and evil very soon acquired political and even military dimensions. Muhammad, it will be recalled, was not only a prophet and a teacher, like the founders of other religions; he was also the head of a polity and of a community, a ruler and a soldier. Hence his struggle involved a state and its armed forces. If the fighters in the war for Islam, the holy war "in the path of God," are fighting for God, it follows that their opponents are fighting against God. And since God is in principle the sovereign, the supreme head of the Islamic state—and the Prophet and, after the Prophet, the caliphs are his vicegerents—then God as sovereign commands the army. The army is God's army and the enemy is God's enemy. The duty of God's soldiers is to dispatch God's enemies as quickly as possible to the place where God will chastise them—that is to say, the afterlife.

Clearly related to this is the basic division of mankind as perceived in Islam. Most, probably all, human societies have a way of distinguishing between themselves and others: insider and outsider, in-group and out-group, kinsman or neighbor and foreigner. These definitions not only define the outsider but also, and perhaps more particularly, help to define and illustrate our perception of ourselves.

In the classical Islamic view, to which many Muslims are beginning to return, the world and all mankind are divided into two: the House of Islam, where the Muslim law and faith prevail, and the rest, known as the House of Unbelief or the House of War, which it is the duty of Muslims ultimately to bring to Islam. But the greater part of the world is still outside Islam, and even inside the Islamic lands, according to the view of the Muslim radicals, the faith of Islam has been undermined and the law of Islam has been abrogated. The obligation of holy war therefore begins at home and continues abroad, against the same infidel enemy.

Like every other civilization known to human history, the Muslim world in its heyday saw itself as the center of truth and enlightenment, surrounded by infidel barbarians whom it would in due course enlighten and civilize. But between the different groups of barbarians there was a crucial difference. The barbarians to the east and the south were polytheists and idolaters, offering no serious threat and no competition at all to Islam. In the north and west, in contrast, Muslims from an early date recognized a genuine rival—a competing world religion, a distinctive civilization inspired by that religion, and an empire that, though much smaller than theirs, was no less ambitious in its claims and aspirations. This was the entity known to itself and others as Christendom, a term that was long almost identical with Europe.

The struggle between these rival systems has now lasted for some fourteen centuries. It began with the advent of Islam, in the seventh century, and has continued virtually to the present day. It has consisted of a long series of attacks and counterattacks, jihads and crusades, conquests and reconquests. For the first thousand years Islam was advancing, Christendom in retreat and under threat. The new faith conquered the old Christian lands of the Levant and North Africa, and invaded Europe, ruling for a while in Sicily, Spain, Portugal, and even parts of France. The attempt by the Crusaders to recover the lost lands of Christendom in the east was held and thrown back, and even the Muslims' loss of southwestern Europe to the Reconquista was amply compensated by the Islamic advance into southeastern Europe, which twice reached as far as Vienna. For the past three hundred years, since the failure of the second Turkish siege of Vienna in 1683 and the rise of the European colonial empires in Asia and Africa, Islam has been on the defensive, and the Christian and post-Christian civilization of Europe and her daughters has brought the whole world, including Islam, within its orbit.

For a long time now there has been a rising tide of rebellion against this Western paramountcy, and a desire to reassert Muslim values and restore Muslim greatness. The Muslim has suffered successive stages of defeat. The first was his loss of domination in the world, to the advancing power of Russia and the West. The second was the under-mining of his authority in his own country, through an invasion of foreign ideas and laws and ways of life and sometimes even foreign rulers or settlers, and the enfranchisement of native non-Muslim elements. The third—the last straw—was the challenge to his mastery in his own house, from emancipated women and rebellious children. It was too much to endure, and the outbreak of rage against these alien, infidel, and incomprehensible forces that had subverted his dominance, disrupted his society, and finally violated the sanctuary of his home was inevitable. It was also natural that this rage should be directed primarily against the millennial enemy and should draw its strength from ancient beliefs and loyalties.

Europe and her daughters? The phrase may seem odd to Americans, whose national myths, since the beginning of their nationhood and even earlier, have usually defined their very identity in opposition to Europe, as something new and radically different from the old European ways. This is not, however, the way that others have seen it; not often in Europe, and hardly ever elsewhere.

Though people of other races and cultures participated, for the most part involuntarily, in the discovery and creation of the Americas, this was, and in the eyes of the rest of the world long remained, a European enterprise, in which Europeans predominated and dominated and to which Europeans gave their languages, their religions, and much of their way of life.

For a very long time voluntary immigration to America was almost exclusively European. There were indeed some who came from the Muslim lands in the Middle East and North Africa, but few were Muslims; most were members of the Christian and to a lesser extent the Jewish minorities in those countries. Their departure for America, and their subsequent presence in America, must have strengthened rather than lessened the European image of America in Muslim eyes.

In the lands of Islam remarkably little was known about America. At first the voyages of discovery aroused some interest; the only surviving copy of Columbus's own map of America is a Turkish translation and adaptation, still preserved in the Topkapi Palace Museum, in Istanbul. A sixteenth-century Turkish geographer's account of the discovery of the New World, titled *The History of Western India*, was one of the first books printed in Turkey. But thereafter interest seems to have waned, and not much is said about America in Turkish, Arabic, or other Muslim languages until a relatively late date. A Moroccan ambassador who was in Spain at the time wrote what must surely be the first Arabic account of the American Revolution. The Sultan of Morocco signed a treaty of peace and friendship with the United States in 1787, and thereafter the new republic had a number of dealings, some friendly, some hostile, most commercial, with other Muslim states. These seem to have had little impact on either side. The American Revolution and the American republic to which it gave birth long remained unnoticed and unknown. Even the small but growing American presence in Muslim lands in the nineteenth century—merchants, consuls, missionaries, and teachers—aroused little or no curiosity, and is almost unmentioned in the Muslim literature and newspapers of the time.

The Second World War, the oil industry, and postwar developments brought many Americans to the Islamic lands; increasing numbers of Muslims also came to America, first as students, then as teachers or businessmen or other visitors, and eventually as immigrants. Cinema and later television brought the American way of life, or at any rate a certain version of it, before countless millions to whom the very name of America had previously been meaningless or unknown. A wide range of American products, particularly in the immediate postwar years, when European competition was virtually eliminated and Japanese competition had not yet arisen, reached into the remotest markets of the Muslim world, winning new customers and, perhaps more important, creating new tastes and ambitions. For some, America represented freedom and justice and opportunity. For many more, it represented wealth and power and success, at a time when these qualities were not regarded as sins or crimes.

And then came the great change, when the leaders of a widespread and widening religious revival sought out and identified their enemies as the enemies of God, and gave them "a local habitation and a name" in the Western Hemisphere. Suddenly, or so it seemed, America had become the archenemy, the incarnation of evil, the diabolic opponent of all that is good, and specifically, for Muslims, of Islam. Why?

Some Familiar Accusations

Among the components in the mood of anti-Westernism, and more especially of anti-Americanism, were certain intellectual influences coming from Europe. One of these was from Germany, where a negative view of America formed part of a school of thought by no means limited to the Nazis but including writers as diverse as Rainer Maria Rilke, Ernst Junger, and Martin Heidegger. In this perception, America was the ultimate example of civilization without culture: rich and comfortable, materially advanced but soulless and artificial; assembled or at best constructed, not grown; mechanical, not organic; technologically complex but lacking the spirituality and vitality of the rooted, human, national cultures of the Germans and other "authentic" peoples. German philosophy, and particularly the philosophy of education, enjoyed a considerable vogue among Arab and some other Muslim intellectuals in the thirties and early forties, and this philosophic anti-Americanism was part of the message.

After the collapse of the Third Reich and the temporary ending of German influence, another philosophy, even more anti-American, took its place—the Soviet version of Marxism, with a denunciation of Western capitalism and of America as its most advanced and dangerous embodiment. And when Soviet influence began to fade, there was yet another to take its place, or at least to supplement its working—the new mystique of Third Worldism, emanating from Western Europe, particularly France, and later also from the United States, and drawing at times on

both these earlier philosophies. This mystique was helped by
the universal human tendency to invent a golden age in the
past, and the specifically European propensity to locate it elsewhere. A new variant of the old golden-age myth placed it in the
Third World, where the innocence of the non-Western Adam and
Eve was ruined by the Western serpent. This view took as
axiomatic the goodness and purity of the East and the wicked-
ness of the West, expanding in an exponential curve of evil from
Western Europe to the United States. These ideas, too, fell on
fertile ground, and won widespread support.

But though these imported philosophies helped to provide intellectual expression for anti-Westernism and
anti-Americanism, they did not cause it, and certainly they do
not explain the widespread anti-Westernism that made so
many in the Middle East and elsewhere in the Islamic world
receptive to such ideas.

It must surely be clear that what won support for such
totally diverse doctrines was not Nazi race theory, which can
have had little appeal for Arabs, or Soviet atheistic communism, which can have had little appeal for Muslims, but rather
their common anti-Westernism. Nazism and communism were
the main forces opposed to the West, both as a way of life and
as a power in the world, and as such they could count on at
least the sympathy if not the support of those who saw in the
West their principal enemy.

But why the hostility in the first place? If we turn from
the general to the specific, there is no lack of individual policies and actions, pursued and taken by individual Western
governments, that have aroused the passionate anger of
Middle Eastern and other Islamic peoples. Yet all too often,

when these policies are abandoned and the problems resolved, there is only a local and temporary alleviation. The French have left Algeria, the British have left Egypt, the Western oil companies have left their oil wells, the westernising Shah has left Iran—yet the generalized resentment of the fundamentalists and other extremists against the West and its friends remains and grows and is not appeased.

The cause most frequently adduced for anti-American feeling among Muslims today is American support for Israel. This support is certainly a factor of importance, increasing with nearness and involvement. But here again there are some oddities, difficult to explain in terms of a single, simple cause. In the early days of the foundation of Israel, while the United States maintained a certain distance, the Soviet Union granted immediate de jure recognition and support, and arms sent from a Soviet satellite, Czechoslovakia, saved the infant state of Israel from defeat and death in its first weeks of life. Yet there seems to have been no great ill will toward the Soviets for these policies, and no corresponding good will toward the United States. In 1956 it was the United States that intervened, forcefully and decisively, to secure the withdrawal of Israeli, British, and French forces from Egypt—yet in the late fifties and sixties it was to the Soviets, not America, that the rulers of Egypt, Syria, Iraq, and other states turned for arms; it was with the Soviet bloc that they formed bonds of solidarity at the United Nations and in the world generally. More recently, the rulers of the Islamic Republic of Iran have offered the most principled and uncompromising denunciation of Israel and Zionism. Yet even these leaders, before as well as after the death of Ayatollah Ruhollah

Khomeini, when they decided for reasons of their own to enter into a dialogue of sorts, found it easier to talk to Jerusalem than to Washington. At the same time, Western hostages in Lebanon, many of them devoted to Arab causes and some of them converts to Islam, are seen and treated by their captors as limbs of the Great Satan.

Another explanation, more often heard from Muslim dissidents, attributes anti-American feeling to American support for hated regimes, seen as reactionary by radicals, as impious by conservatives, as corrupt and tyrannical by both. This accusation has some plausibility, and could help to explain why an essentially inner-directed, often anti-nationalist movement should turn against a foreign power. But it does not suffice, especially since support for such regimes has been limited both in extent and—as the Shah discovered—in effectiveness.

Clearly, something deeper is involved than these specific grievances, numerous and important as they may be—something deeper that turns every disagreement into a problem and makes every problem insoluble.

This revulsion against America, more generally against the West, is by no means limited to the Muslim world; nor have Muslims, with the exception of the Iranian mullahs and their disciples elsewhere, experienced and exhibited the more virulent forms of this feeling. The mood of disillusionment and hostility has affected many other parts of the world, and has even reached some elements in the United States. It is from these last, speaking for themselves and claiming to speak for the oppressed peoples of the Third World, that the most widely publicized explanations—and justifications—of this rejection of Western civilization and its values have of late been heard.

The accusations are familiar. We of the West are accused of sexism, racism, and imperialism, institutionalized in patriarchy and slavery, tyranny and exploitation. To these charges, and to others as heinous, we have no option but to plead guilty—not as Americans, nor yet as Westerners, but simply as human beings, as members of the human race. In none of these sins are we the only sinners, and in some of them we are very far from being the worst. The treatment of women in the Western world, and more generally in Christendom, has always been unequal and often oppressive, but even at its worst it was rather better than the rule of polygamy and concubinage that has otherwise been the almost universal lot of womankind on this planet.

Is racism, then, the main grievance? Certainly the word figures prominently in publicity addressed to Western, Eastern European, and some Third World audiences. It figures less prominently in what is written and published for home consumption, and has become a generalized and meaningless term of abuse—rather like "fascism," which is nowadays imputed to opponents even by spokesmen for one-party, nationalist dictatorships of various complexions and shirt colors.

Slavery is today universally denounced as an offense against humanity, but within living memory it has been practiced and even defended as a necessary institution, established and regulated by divine law. The peculiarity of the peculiar institution, as Americans once called it, lay not in its existence but in its abolition. Westerners were the first to break the consensus of acceptance and to outlaw slavery, first at home, then in the other territories they controlled, and finally wherever in the world they were able to exercise power or influence—in a word, by means of imperialism.

Is imperialism, then, the grievance? Some Western powers, and in a sense Western civilization as a whole, have certainly been guilty of imperialism, but are we really to believe that in the expansion of Western Europe there was a quality of moral delinquency lacking in such earlier, relatively innocent expansions as those of the Arabs or the Mongols or the Ottomans, or in more recent expansions such as that which brought the rulers of Muscovy to the Baltic, the Black Sea, the Caspian, the Hindu Kush, and the Pacific Ocean? In having practiced sexism, racism, and imperialism, the West was merely following the common practice of mankind through the millennia of recorded history. Where it is distinct from all other civilizations is in having recognized, named, and tried, not entirely without success, to remedy these historic diseases. And that is surely a matter for congratulation, not condemnation. We do not hold Western medical science in general, or Dr. Parkinson and Dr. Alzheimer in particular, responsible for the diseases they diagnosed and to which they gave their names.

Of all these offenses the one that is most widely, frequently, and vehemently denounced is undoubtedly imperialism—sometimes just Western, sometimes Eastern (that is, Soviet) and Western alike. But the way this term is used in the literature of Islamic fundamentalists often suggests that it may not carry quite the same meaning for them as for its Western critics. In many of these writings the term "imperialist" is given a distinctly religious significance, being used in association, and sometimes interchangeably, with "missionary," and denoting a form of attack that includes the Crusades as well as the modern colonial empires. One also sometimes gets the impression that the offense of imperialism is not—as for Western critics—the domination by one people over another but rather the allocation of roles in this relationship. What is truly evil and unacceptable is the domination of infidels over true believers. For true believers to rule misbelievers is proper and natural, since this provides for the maintenance of the holy law, and gives the misbelievers both the opportunity and the incentive to embrace the true faith. But for misbelievers to rule over true believers is blasphemous and unnatural, since it leads to the corruption of religion and morality in society, and to the flouting or even the abrogation of God's law. This may help us to understand the current troubles in such diverse places as Ethiopian Eritrea, Indian Kashmir, Chinese Sinkiang, and Yugoslav Kosovo, in all of which Muslim populations are ruled by non-Muslim governments. It may also explain why spokesmen for the new Muslim minorities in Western Europe demand for Islam a degree of legal protection which those countries no longer give to Christianity and have never given to Judaism. Nor, of course, did the governments of the countries of origin of these Muslim spokesmen ever accord such protection to religions other than their own. In their perception, there is no contradiction in these attitudes. The true faith, based on God's final revelation, must be protected from insult and abuse; other faiths, being either false or incomplete, have no right to any such protection.

There are other difficulties in the way of accepting imperialism as an explanation of Muslim hostility, even if we define imperialism narrowly and specifically, as the invasion and domination of Muslim countries by non-Muslims. If the hostility is directed against imperialism in that sense, why has it been so much stronger against Western Europe, which has relinquished all its Muslim possessions and dependencies, than against Russia, which still rules, with no light hand, over many millions of reluctant Muslim subjects and over ancient Muslim cities and countries? And why should it include the United States, which, apart from a brief interlude in the Muslim-minority area of the Philippines, has never ruled any Muslim population? The last surviving European empire with Muslim subjects, that of the Soviet Union, far from being the target of criticism and attack, has been almost exempt. Even the most recent repressions of Muslim revolts in the southern and central Asian republics of the USSR incurred no more than relatively mild words of expostulation, coupled with a disclaimer of any desire to interfere in what are quaintly called the "internal affairs" of the USSR and a request for the preservation of order and tranquillity on the frontier.

One reason for this somewhat surprising restraint is to be found in the nature of events in Soviet Azerbaijan. Islam is obviously an important and potentially a growing element in the Azerbaijani sense of identity, but it is not at present a dominant element, and the Azerbaijani movement has more in common with the liberal patriotism of Europe than with Islamic fundamentalism. Such a movement would not arouse the sympathy of the rulers of the Islamic Republic. It might even alarm them, since a genuinely democratic national state run by the people of Soviet Azerbaijan would exercise a powerful attraction on their kinsmen immediately to the south, in Iranian Azerbaijan.

Another reason for this relative lack of concern for the 50 million or more Muslims under Soviet rule may be a calculation of risk and advantage. The Soviet Union is near, along the northern frontiers of Turkey, Iran, and Afghanistan; America and even Western Europe are far away. More to the point, it has not hitherto been the practice of the Soviets to quell disturbances with water cannon and rubber bullets, with TV cameras in attendance, or to release arrested persons on bail and allow them access to domestic and foreign media. The Soviets do not interview their harshest critics on prime time, or tempt them with teaching, lecturing, and writing engagements. On the contrary, their ways of indicating displeasure with criticism can often be quite disagreeable.

But fear of reprisals, though no doubt important, is not the only or perhaps even the principal reason for the relatively minor place assigned to the Soviet Union, as compared with the West, in the demonology of fundamentalism. After all, the great social and intellectual and economic changes that have transformed most of the Islamic world, and given rise to such commonly denounced Western evils as consumerism and secularism, emerged from the West, not from the Soviet Union. No one could accuse the Soviets of consumerism; their materialism is philosophic—to be precise, dialectical—and has little or nothing to do in practice with providing the good things of life. Such provision represents another kind of materialism, often designated by its opponents as crass. It is associated with the capitalist West and not with the communist East, which has practiced, or at least imposed on its subjects, a degree of austerity that would impress a Sufi saint.

Nor were the Soviets, until very recently, vulnerable to charges of secularism, the other great fundamentalist accusation against the West. Though atheist, they were not godless, and had in fact created an elaborate state apparatus to impose the worship of their gods—an apparatus with its own orthodoxy, a hierarchy to define and enforce it, and an armed inquisition to detect and extirpate heresy. The separation of religion from the state does not mean the establishment of irreligion by the state, still less the forcible imposition of an anti-religious philosophy. Soviet secularism, like Soviet consumerism, holds no temptation for the Muslim masses, and is losing what appeal it had for Muslim intellectuals. More than ever before it is Western capitalism and democracy that provide an authentic and attractive alternative to traditional ways of thought and life. Fundamentalist leaders are not mistaken in seeing in Western civilization the greatest challenge to the way of life that they wish to retain or restore for their people.

A Clash of Civilizations

The origins of secularism in the West may be found in two circumstances—in early Christian teachings and, still more, experience, which created two institutions, Church and State; and in later Christian conflicts, which drove the two apart. Muslims, too, had their religious disagreements, but there was nothing remotely approaching the ferocity of the Christian struggles between Protestants and Catholics, which devastated Christian Europe in the sixteenth and seventeenth centuries and finally drove Christians in desperation to evolve a doctrine of the separation of religion from the state. Only by depriving religious institutions of coercive power, it seemed, could Christendom restrain the murderous intolerance and persecution that Christians had visited on followers of other religions and, most of all, on those who professed other forms of their own.

Muslims experienced no such need and evolved no such doctrine. There was no need for secularism in Islam, and even its pluralism was very different from that of the pagan Roman Empire, so vividly described by Edward Gibbon when he remarked that "the various modes of worship, which prevailed in the Roman world, were all considered by the people, as equally true; by the philosopher, as equally false; and by the magistrate, as equally useful." Islam was never prepared, either in theory or in practice, to accord full equality to those who held other beliefs and practiced other forms of worship. It did, however, accord to the holders of partial truth a degree of practical as well as theoretical tolerance rarely paralleled in the Christian world until the West adopted a measure of secularism in the late-seventeenth and eighteenth centuries.

At first the Muslim response to Western civilization was one of admiration and emulation—an immense respect for the achievements of the West, and a desire to imitate and adopt them. This desire arose from a keen and growing awareness of the weakness, poverty, and backwardness of the Islamic world as compared with the advancing West. The disparity first became apparent on the battlefield but soon spread to other areas of human activity. Muslim writers observed and described the wealth and power of the West, its science and technology, its manufactures, and its forms of government. For a time the secret of Western success was seen to lie in two achievements: economic advancement and especially industry; political institutions and especially freedom. Several generations of reformers and modernizers tried to adapt these and introduce them to their own countries, in the hope that they would thereby be able to achieve equality with the West and perhaps restore their lost superiority.

In our own time this mood of admiration and emulation has, among many Muslims, given way to one of hostility and rejection. In part this mood is surely due to a feeling of humiliation—a growing awareness, among the heirs of an old, proud, and long dominant civilization, of having been over-taken, overborne, and overwhelmed by those whom they regarded as their inferiors. In part this mood is due to events in the Western world itself. One factor of major importance was certainly the impact of two great suicidal wars, in which Western civilization tore itself apart, bringing untold destruction to its own and other peoples, and in which the belligerents conducted an immense propaganda effort, in the Islamic world and elsewhere, to discredit and undermine each other. The message they brought found many listeners, who were all the more ready to respond in that their own experience of Western ways was not happy. The introduction of Western commercial, financial, and industrial methods did indeed bring great wealth, but it accrued to transplanted Westerners and members of Westernized minorities, and to only a few among the mainstream Muslim population. In time these few became more numerous, but they remained isolated from the masses, differing from them even in their dress and style of life. Inevitably they were seen as agents of and col-laborators with what was once again regarded as a hostile world. Even the political institutions that had come from the West were discredited, being judged not by their Western originals but by their local imitations, installed by enthusiastic Muslim reformers. These, operating in a situation beyond their control, using imported and inappropriate methods that they did not fully understand, were unable to cope with the rapidly developing crises and were one by one overthrown. For vast numbers of Middle Easterners, Western-style economic methods brought poverty, Western-style political institutions brought tyranny, even Western-style warfare brought defeat. It is hardly surprising that so many were willing to listen to voices telling them that the old Islamic ways were best and that their only salvation was to throw aside the pagan innovations of the reformers and return to the True Path that God had prescribed for his people.

Ultimately, the struggle of the fundamentalists is against two enemies, secularism and modernism. The war against secularism is conscious and explicit, and there is by now a whole literature denouncing secularism as an evil neo-pagan force in the modern world and attributing it variously to the Jews, the West, and the United States. The war against modernity is for the most part neither conscious nor explicit, and is directed against the whole process of change that has taken place in the Islamic world in the past century or more and has transformed the political, economic, social, and even cultural structures of Muslim countries. Islamic fundamentalism has given an aim and a form to the otherwise aimless and formless resentment and anger of the Muslim masses at the forces that have devalued their traditional values and loyalties and, in the final analysis, robbed them of their beliefs, their aspirations, their dignity, and to an increasing extent even their livelihood.

There is something in the religious culture of Islam which inspired, in even the humblest peasant or peddler, a dignity and a courtesy toward others never exceeded and rarely equalled in other civilizations. And yet, in moments of upheaval and disruption, when the deeper passions are stirred, this dignity and courtesy toward others can give way to an explosive mixture of rage and hatred which impels even the government of an ancient and civilized country—even the spokesman of a great spiritual and ethical religion—to espouse kidnapping and assassination, and try to find, in the life of their Prophet, approval and indeed precedent for such actions

The instinct of the masses is not false in locating the ultimate source of these cataclysmic changes in the West and in attributing the disruption of their old way of life to the impact of Western domination, Western influence, or Western precept and example. And since the United States is the legitimate heir of European civilization and the recognized and unchallenged leader of the West, the United States has inherited the resulting grievances and become the focus for the pent-up hate and anger. Two examples may suffice. In November of 1979 an angry mob attacked and burned the U.S. Embassy in Islamabad, Pakistan. The stated cause of the crowd's anger was the seizure of the Great Mosque in Mecca by a group of Muslim dissidents—an event in which there was no American involvement whatsoever. Almost ten years later, in February of 1989, again in Islamabad, the USIS center was attacked by angry crowds,

this time to protest the publication of Salman Rushdie's
Satanic Verses. Rushdie is a British citizen of Indian birth,
and his book had been published five months previously in
England. But what provoked the mob's anger, and also the
Ayatollah Khomeini's subsequent pronouncement of a death
sentence on the author, was the publication of the book in
the United States.

It should by now be clear that we are facing a mood and
a movement far transcending the level of issues and policies
and the governments that pursue them. This is no less than a
clash of civilizations—the perhaps irrational but surely historic reaction of an ancient rival against our Judeo-Christian
heritage, our secular present, and the worldwide expansion of
both. It is crucially important that we on our side should not
be provoked into an equally historic but also equally irrational
reaction against that rival.

Not all the ideas imported from the West by Western
intruders or native Westernizers have been rejected. Some
have been accepted by even the most radical Islamic fundamentalists, usually without acknowledgment of source, and
suffering a sea change into something rarely rich but often
strange. One such was political freedom, with the associated
notions and practices of representation, election, and constitu-
tional government. Even the Islamic Republic of Iran has a
written constitution and an elected assembly, as well as a kind
of episcopate, for none of which is there any prescription in
Islamic teaching or any precedent in the Islamic past. All
these institutions are clearly adapted from Western models.
Muslim states have also retained many of the cultural and
social customs of the West and the symbols that express them,

such as the form and style of male (and to a much lesser extent female) clothing, notably in the military. The use of Western-invented guns and tanks and planes is a military necessity, but the continued use of fitted tunics and peaked caps is a cultural choice. From constitutions to Coca-Cola, from tanks and television to T-shirts, the symbols and artifacts, and through them the ideas, of the West have retained—even strengthened—their appeal.

The movement nowadays called fundamentalism is not the only Islamic tradition. There are others, more tolerant, more open, that helped to inspire the great achievements of Islamic civilization in the past, and we may hope that these other traditions will in time prevail. But before this issue is decided there will be a hard struggle, in which we of the West can do little or nothing. Even the attempt might do harm, for these are issues that Muslims must decide among themselves. And in the meantime we must take great care on all sides to avoid the danger of a new era of religious wars, arising from the exacerbation of differences and the revival of ancient prejudices.

To this end we must strive to achieve a better appreciation of other religious and political cultures, through the study of their history, their literature, and their achievements. At the same time, we may hope that they will try to achieve a better understanding of ours, and especially that they will understand and respect, even if they do not choose to adopt for themselves, our Western perception of the proper relationship between religion and politics. To describe this perception I shall end as I began, with a quotation from an American President, this time not the justly celebrated Thomas Jefferson but the somewhat unjustly neglected John Tyler, who, in a letter dated July 10, 1843, gave eloquent and indeed prophetic expression to the principle of religious freedom:

The United States have adventured upon a great and noble experiment, which is believed to have been hazarded in the absence of all previous precedent—that of total separation of Church and State. No religious establishment by law exists among us. The conscience is left free from all restraint and each is permitted to worship his Maker after his own judgement. The offices of the Government are open alike to all. No tithes are levied to support an established Hierarchy, nor is the fallible judgement of man set up as the sure and infallible creed of faith. The Mahommedan, if he will to come among us would have the privilege guaranteed to him by the constitution to worship according to the Koran; and the East Indian might erect a shrine to Brahma if it so pleased him. Such is the spirit of toleration inculcated by our political Institutions . . . The Hebrew persecuted and down trodden in other regions takes up his abode among us with none to make him afraid . . . and the Aegis of the Government is over him to defend and protect him. Such is the great experiment which we have tried, and such are the happy fruits which have resulted from it; our system of free government would be imperfect without it.

The body may be oppressed and manacled and yet survive; but if the mind of man be fettered, its energies and faculties perish, and what remains is of the earth, earthly. Mind should be free as the light or as the air.

———■———

Samuel P. Huntington is a professor of international studies at Harvard and was a member of the National Security Council during the presidency of Jimmy Carter (1977–1981). He was also the founder and editor of Foreign Policy, *an influential foreign-affairs journal. The selection below is from Huntington's article "The Clash of Civilizations?" The article appeared in the summer 1993 issue of* Foreign Affairs *and, according to its editors, "stirred up more discussion in three years than anything they had published since the 1940s."*

Huntington's theory is that with the end of the Cold War, "the most pervasive, important, and dangerous conflicts will not be between social classes, rich and poor, or other economically defined groups, but between peoples belonging to different cultural entities." These cultural entities, according to Huntington, will be defined by differences in "philosophical assumptions, underlying values, social relations, customs, and overall outlooks on life." Chief among these is religion. As people increasingly define themselves in terms of ethnicity and religion, Huntington sees an increased likelihood of an "us versus them" mentality defining relationships between different groups. As the world's Islamist movements become increasingly "supranational" in character (see the last selection in this chapter), the implications of Huntington's thesis

*for relations between Islam and the West become even
more provocative. —JJ*

From "The Clash of Civilizations?"
by Samuel P. Huntington
Foreign Affairs, **Summer 1993**

During the cold war the world was divided into the First,
Second and Third Worlds. Those divisions are no longer relevant. It is far more meaningful now to group countries not in
terms of their political or economic systems or in terms of
their level of economic development but rather in terms of their
culture and civilization.

What do we mean when we talk of a civilization? A civilization is a cultural entity. Villages, regions, ethnic groups,
nationalities, religious groups, all have distinct cultures at different levels of cultural heterogeneity. The culture of a village
in southern Italy may be different from that of a village in
northern Italy, but both will share in a common Italian culture
that distinguishes them from German villages. European communities, in turn, will share cultural features that distinguish
them from Arab or Chinese communities. Arabs, Chinese and
Westerners, however, are not part of any broader cultural
entity. They constitute civilizations. A civilization is thus the
highest cultural grouping of people and the broadest level of
cultural identity people have short of that which distinguishes
humans from other species. It is defined both by common
objective elements, such as language, history, religion, customs, institutions, and by the subjective self-identification of
people. People have levels of identity: a resident of Rome may

define himself with varying degrees of intensity as a Roman, an Italian, a Catholic, a Christian, a European, a Westerner. The civilization to which he belongs is the broadest level of identification with which he intensely identifies. People can and do redefine their identities and, as a result, the composition and boundaries of civilizations change.

Civilizations may involve a large number of people, as with China ("a civilization pretending to be a state," as Lucian Pye put it), or a very small number of people, such as the Anglophone Caribbean. A civilization may include several nation states, as is the case with Western, Latin American and Arab civilizations, or only one, as is the case with Japanese civilization. Civilizations obviously blend and overlap, and may include subcivilizations. Western civilization has two major variants, European and North American, and Islam has its Arab, Turkic and Malay subdivisions. Civilizations are nonetheless meaningful entities, and while the lines between them are seldom sharp, they are real. Civilizations are dynamic; they rise and fall; they divide and merge. And, as any student of history knows, civilizations disappear and are buried in the sands of time.

Westerners tend to think of nation states as the principal actors in global affairs. They have been that, however, for only a few centuries. The broader reaches of human history have been the history of civilizations. In *A Study of History*, Arnold Toynbee identified 21 major civilizations; only six of them exist in the contemporary world.

Why Civilizations Will Clash

Civilization identity will be increasingly important in the future, and the world will be shaped in large measure by the interactions among seven or eight major civilizations. These include Western, Confucian, Japanese, Islamic, Hindu, Slavic-Orthodox, Latin American and possibly African civilization. The most important conflicts of the future will occur along the cultural fault lines separating these civilizations from one another.

Why will this be the case?

First, differences among civilizations are not only real; they are basic. Civilizations are differentiated from each other by history, language, culture, tradition and, most important, religion. The people of different civilizations have different views on the relations between God and man, the individual and the group, the citizen and the state, parents and children, husband and wife, as well as differing views of the relative importance of rights and responsibilities, liberty and authority, equality and hierarchy. These differences are the product of centuries. They will not soon disappear. They are far more fundamental than differences among political ideologies and political regimes. Differences do not necessarily mean conflict, and conflict does not necessarily, mean violence. Over the centuries, however, differences among civilizations have generated the most prolonged and the most violent conflicts.

Second, the world is becoming a smaller place. The interactions between peoples of different civilizations are increasing; these increasing interactions intensify civilization consciousness and awareness of differences between civilizations and commonalities within civilizations. North African immigration to France generates hostility among Frenchmen and at the same time increased receptivity to immigration by "good" European Catholic Poles. Americans react far more negatively to Japanese investment than to larger investments from Canada and European countries. Similarly, as Donald Horowitz has pointed out, "An Ibo may be . . . an Owerri Ibo or an Onitsha Ibo in what was the Eastern region of Nigeria. In Lagos, he is simply an Ibo. In London, he is a Nigerian. In New York, he is an African." The interactions among peoples of different civilizations enhance the civilization-consciousness of people that, in turn, invigorates differences and animosities stretching or thought to stretch back deep into history.

Third, the processes of economic modernization and social change throughout the world are separating people from longstanding local identities. They also weaken the nation state as a source of identity. In much of the world religion has moved in to fill this gap, often in the form of movements that are labeled "fundamentalist." Such movements are found in Western Christianity, Judaism, Buddhism and Hinduism, as well as in Islam. In most countries and most religions the people active in fundamentalist movements are young, college-educated, middle-class technicians, professionals and business persons. The "unsecularization of the world," George Weigel has remarked, "is one of the dominant social facts of life in the late twentieth century." The revival of religion, "la revanche de Dieu," as Gilles Kepel labeled it, provides a basis for identity and commitment that transcends national boundaries and unites civilizations.

Fourth, the growth of civilization-consciousness is enhanced by the dual role of the West. On the one hand, the West is at a peak of power. At the same time, however, and perhaps as a result, a return to the roots phenomenon is occurring among non-Western civilizations. Increasingly one hears references to trends toward a turning inward and "Asianization" in Japan, the end of the Nehru legacy and the "Hinduization" of India, the failure of Western ideas of socialism and nationalism and hence "re-Islamization" of the Middle East, and now a debate over Westernization versus Russianization in Boris Yeltsin's country. A West at the peak of its power confronts non-Wests that increasingly have the desire, the will and the resources to shape the world in non-Western ways.

In the past, the elites of non-Western societies were usually the people who were most involved with the West, had been educated at Oxford, the Sorbonne or Sandhurst, and had absorbed Western attitudes and values. At the same time, the populace in non-Western countries often remained deeply imbued with the indigenous culture. Now, however, these relationships are being reversed. A de-Westernization and indigenization of elites is occurring in many non-Western countries at the same time that Western, usually American, cultures, styles and habits become more popular among the mass of the people.

Fifth, cultural characteristics and differences are less mutable and hence less easily compromised and resolved than political and economic ones. In the former Soviet Union, communists can become democrats, the rich can become poor and the poor rich, but Russians cannot become Estonians and Azeris cannot become Armenians. In class and ideological conflicts, the key question was "Which side are you on?" and people could and did choose sides and change sides. In conflicts between civilizations, the question is "What are you?" That is a given that cannot be changed. And as we know, from

Bosnia to the Caucasus to the Sudan, the wrong answer to that question can mean a bullet in the head. Even more than ethnicity, religion discriminates sharply and exclusively among people. A person can be half-French and half-Arab and simultaneously even a citizen of two countries. It is more difficult to be half-Catholic and half-Muslim.

Finally, economic regionalism is increasing. The proportions of total trade that were intraregional rose between 1980 and 1989 from 51 percent to 59 percent in Europe, 33 percent to 37 percent in East Asia, and 32 percent to 36 percent in North America. The importance of regional economic blocs is likely to continue to increase in the future. On the one hand, successful economic regionalism will reinforce civilization-consciousness. On the other hand, economic regionalism may succeed only when it is rooted in a common civilization. The European Community rests on the shared foundation of European culture and Western Christianity. The success of the North American Free Trade Area depends on the convergence now underway of Mexican, Canadian and American cultures. Japan, in contrast, faces difficulties in creating a comparable economic entity in East Asia because Japan is a society and civilization unique to itself. However strong the trade and investment links Japan may develop with other East Asian countries, its cultural differences with those countries inhibit and perhaps preclude its promoting regional economic integration like that in Europe and North America . . .

As people define their identity in ethnic and religious terms, they are likely to see an "us" versus "them" relation existing between themselves and people of different ethnicity or religion. The end of ideologically defined states in

Eastern Europe and the former Soviet Union permits traditional ethnic identities and animosities to come to the fore. Differences in culture and religion create differences over policy issues, ranging from human rights to immigration to trade and commerce to the environment. Geographical propinquity gives rise to conflicting territorial claims from Bosnia to Mindanao. Most important, the efforts of the West to promote its values of democracy and liberalism as universal values, to maintain its military predominance and to advance its economic interests engender countering responses from other civilizations. Decreasingly able to mobilize support and form coalitions on the basis of ideology, governments and groups will increasingly attempt to mobilize support by appealing to common religion and civilization identity.

The clash of civilizations thus occurs at two levels. At the micro-level, adjacent groups along the fault lines between civilizations struggle, often violently, over the control of territory and each other. At the macro-level, states from different civilizations compete for relative military and economic power, struggle over the control of international institutions and third parties, and competitively promote their particular political and religious values.

—■—

Described by Esquire *magazine as "the most influential foreign policy adviser of his generation," Fareed Zakaria is a former managing editor of* Foreign Affairs *and current editor of* Newsweek International. *He is also a columnist for* Newsweek *and the* Washington Post.

The selection below is from Zakaria's article "The Politics of Rage: Why Do They Hate Us?" The article appeared in Newsweek *shortly after the September 11 attack. In it, Zakaria attributes the increasing hostility in relations between Islam and the West to the rise of Islamist movements and calls for the United States to carry out reform in the Islamic world. —JJ*

From "The Politics of Rage: Why Do They Hate Us?"
by Fareed Zakaria
***Newsweek*, October 15, 2001**

To the question "Why do the terrorists hate us?" Americans could be pardoned for answering, "Why should we care?" The immediate reaction to the murder of 5,000 innocents is anger, not analysis. Yet anger will not be enough to get us through what is sure to be a long struggle. For that we will need answers. The ones we have heard so far have been comforting but familiar. We stand for freedom and they hate it. We are rich and they envy us. We are strong and they resent this. All of which is true. But there are billions of poor and weak and oppressed people around the world. They don't turn planes into bombs. They don't blow themselves up to kill thousands of civilians. If envy were the cause of terrorism, Beverly Hills, Fifth Avenue and Mayfair would have become morgues long ago. There is something stronger at work here than deprivation and jealousy. Something that can move men to kill but also to die.

Osama bin Laden has an answer—religion. For him and his followers, this is a holy war between Islam and the Western world. Most Muslims disagree. Every Islamic country in the world has condemned the attacks of Sept. 11. To many, bin Laden belongs to a long line of extremists who have invoked religion to justify mass murder and spur men to suicide. The words "thug," "zealot" and "assassin" all come from ancient terror cults—Hindu, Jewish and Muslim, respectively—that believed they were doing the work of God. The terrorist's mind is its own place, and like Milton's Satan, can make a hell of heaven, a heaven of hell. Whether it is the Unabomber, Aum Shinrikyo or Baruch Goldstein (who killed scores of unarmed Muslims in Hebron), terrorists are almost always misfits who place their own twisted morality above mankind's.

But bin Laden and his followers are not an isolated cult like Aum Shinrikyo or the Branch Davidians or demented loners like Timothy McVeigh and the Unabomber. They come out of a culture that reinforces their hostility, distrust and hatred of the West—and of America in particular. This culture does not condone terrorism but fuels the fanaticism that is at its heart. To say that Al Qaeda is a fringe group may be reassuring, but it is false. Read the Arab press in the aftermath of the attacks and you will detect a not-so-hidden admiration for bin Laden. Or consider this from the Pakistani newspaper *The Nation*:

"September 11 was not mindless terrorism for terrorism's sake. It was reaction and revenge, even retribution." Why else is America's response to the terror attacks so deeply constrained by fears of an "Islamic backlash" on the streets? Pakistan will dare not allow Washington the use of its bases. Saudi Arabia trembles at the thought of having to help us publicly. Egypt pleads that our strikes be as limited as possible. The problem is not that Osama bin Laden believes that this is a religious war against America. It's that millions of people across the Islamic world seem to agree.

This awkward reality has led some in the West to dust off old essays and older prejudices predicting a "clash of civilizations" between the West and Islam. The historian Paul Johnson has argued that Islam is intrinsically an intolerant and violent religion. Other scholars have disagreed, pointing out that Islam condemns the slaughter of innocents and prohibits suicide. Nothing will be solved by searching for "true Islam" or quoting the Quran. The Quran is a vast, vague book, filled with poetry and contradictions (much like the Bible).

You can find in it condemnations of war and incitements to struggle, beautiful expressions of tolerance and stern strictures against unbelievers. Quotations from it usually tell us more about the person who selected the passages than about Islam. Every religion is compatible with the best and the worst of humankind. Through its long history, Christianity has supported inquisitions and anti-Semitism, but also human rights and social welfare.

Searching the history books is also of limited value. From the Crusades of the 11th century to the Turkish expansion of the 15th century to the colonial era in the early 20th century, Islam and the West have often battled militarily. This tension has existed for hundreds of years, during which there have been many periods of peace and even harmony. Until the 1950s, for example, Jews and Christians lived peaceably under Muslim rule. In fact, Bernard Lewis, the pre-eminent historian of Islam, has argued that for much of history religious minorities did better under Muslim rulers than they did under Christian ones.

All that has changed in the past few decades. So surely the relevant question we must ask is, Why are we in a particularly difficult phase right now? What has gone wrong in the world of Islam that explains not the conquest of Constantinople in 1453 or the siege of Vienna of 1683 but September 11, 2001?

Let us first peer inside that vast Islamic world. Many of the largest Muslim countries in the world show little of this anti-American rage. The biggest, Indonesia, had, until the recent Asian economic crisis, been diligently following Washington's advice on economics, with impressive results. The second and third most populous Muslim countries, Pakistan and Bangladesh, have mixed Islam and modernity with some success. While both countries are impoverished, both have voted a woman into power as prime minister, before most Western countries have done so. Next is Turkey, the sixth largest Muslim country in the world, a flawed but functioning secular democracy and a close ally of the West (being a member of NATO).

Only when you get to the Middle East do you see in lurid colors all the dysfunctions that people conjure up when they think of Islam today. In Iran, Egypt, Syria, Iraq, Jordan, the occupied territories and the Persian Gulf, the resurgence of Islamic fundamentalism is virulent, and a raw anti-Americanism seems to be everywhere. This is the land of suicide bombers, flag-burners and fiery mullahs. As we strike Afghanistan it is worth remembering that not a single Afghan has been tied to a terrorist attack against the United States.

Afghanistan is the campground from which an Arab army is battling America. But even the Arab rage at America is relatively recent. In the 1950s and 1960s it seemed unimaginable that the United States and the Arab world would end up locked in a cultural clash. Egypt's most powerful journalist, Mohamed Heikal, described the mood at the time: "The whole picture of the United States . . . was a glamorous one. Britain and France were fading, hated empires. The Soviet Union was 5,000 miles away and the ideology of communism was anathema to the Muslim religion. But America had emerged from World War II richer, more powerful and more appealing than ever." I first traveled to the Middle East in the early 1970s, and even then the image of America was of a glistening, approachable modernity: fast cars, Hilton hotels and Coca-Cola. Something happened in these lands. To understand the roots of anti-American rage in the Middle East, we need to plumb not the past 300 years of history but the past 30 . . .

It turns out that modernization takes more than strongmen and oil money. Importing foreign stuff—Cadillacs, Gulfstreams and McDonald's—is easy. Importing the inner stuffings of modern society—a free market, political parties, accountability and the rule of law—is difficult and dangerous. The gulf states, for example, have gotten modernization lite, with the goods and even the workers imported from abroad. Nothing was homegrown; nothing is even now. As for politics, the gulf governments offered their people a bargain: we will bribe you with wealth, but in return let us stay in power. It was the inverse slogan of the American revolution—no taxation, but no representation either.

The new age of globalization has hit the Arab world in a very strange way. Its societies are open enough to be disrupted by modernity, but not so open that they can ride the wave. They see the television shows, the fast foods and the fizzy drinks. But they don't see genuine liberalization in the society, with increased opportunities and greater openness. Globalization in the Arab world is the critic's caricature of globalization—a slew of Western products and billboards with little else. For some in their societies it means more things to buy. For the regimes it is an unsettling, dangerous phenomenon. As a result, the people they rule can look at globalization but for the most part not touch it.

America stands at the center of this world of globalization. It seems unstoppable. If you close the borders, America comes in through the mail. If you censor the mail, it appears in the fast food and faded jeans. If you ban the products, it seeps in through satellite television. Americans are so comfortable with global capitalism and consumer culture that we cannot fathom just how revolutionary these forces are.

Disoriented young men, with one foot in the old world and another in the new, now look for a purer, simpler alternative. Fundamentalism searches for such people everywhere; it, too, has been globalized. One can now find men in Indonesia who regard the Palestinian cause as their own. (Twenty years ago an Indonesian Muslim would barely have known where Palestine was.) Often they learned about this path away from the West while they were in the West. As did Mohamed Atta, the Hamburg-educated engineer who drove the first plane into the World Trade Center.

The Arab world has a problem with its Attas in more than one sense. Globalization has caught it at a bad demographic moment. Arab societies are going through a massive youth bulge, with more than half of most countries' populations under the age of 25. Young men, often better educated than their parents, leave their traditional villages to find work. They arrive in noisy, crowded cities like Cairo, Beirut and Damascus or go to work in the oil states. (Almost 10 percent of Egypt's working population worked in the gulf at one point.) In their new world they see great disparities of wealth and the disorienting effects of modernity; most unsettlingly, they see women, unveiled and in public places, taking buses, eating in cafes and working alongside them.

A huge influx of restless young men in any country is bad news. When accompanied by even small economic and social change, it usually produces a new politics of protest. In the past, societies in these circumstances have fallen prey to a search for revolutionary solutions. (France went through a youth bulge just before the French Revolution, as did Iran before its 1979 revolution.) In the case of the Arab world, this revolution has taken the form of an Islamic resurgence.

———■———

Olivier Roy is research director at the French National Center for Scientific Research, where his work has focused on the Islamic world. In the brief article reprinted here, Roy outlines the ways in which modern Islamist movements, which he characterizes as supra-national (transcending national boundaries) in character, are transforming the contemporary geopolitical landscape. He notes that these Islamist movements are

*inextricably linked to the economic phenomenon known
as globalization and therefore share kinship with
Christian fundamentalist movements elsewhere in the
world, including the United States.* —JJ

"Neo-Fundamentalism"
by Olivier Roy
Social Science Resource Council, circa 2002

More than twenty years after the success of the Islamic
revolution in Iran, the wave of Islamic radicalism that has
engulfed the Middle East since the late 1970s is taking a different course. The mainstream Islamist movements have
shifted from the struggle for a supranational Muslim community into a kind of Islamo-nationalism: they want to be fully
recognized as legitimate actors on the domestic political
scene, and have largely given up the supranational agenda
that was part of their ideology. On the other hand, the policy
of conservative re-Islamization implemented by many states,
even secular ones, in order to undercut the Islamist opposition and to regain some religious legitimacy has backfired. It
has produced a new brand of Islamic fundamentalism, ideologically conservative but at times politically radical. This
neo-fundamentalism is largely de-linked from states' policy
and strategy. At first glance it is less politically minded than
the Islamist movements—less concerned with defining what a
true Islamic State should be than with the implementation of
shariat (Islamic law). Though the movement is basically a
sociocultural phenomenon, it has also produced an extremist
expression which is embodied in loose peripheral networks,

such as the organization Al Qaeda, headed by Osama bin Laden, responsible for the destruction of the World Trade Center on 11 September 2001. Consequently, international Islamic terrorism has shifted from state-sponsored actions or actions against domestic targets toward a de-territorialized, supranational and largely uprooted activism. Nevertheless the strategic impact of these new movements is limited by the very fact that they have such scarce roots in the states' domestic politics. However, this is not the case in Pakistan and Afghanistan, which are now the hotbed of contemporary Islamic fundamentalism.

"Islamism" is the brand of modern political Islamic fundamentalism which claims to recreate a true Islamic society, not simply by imposing the shariat, but by establishing first an Islamic state through political action. Islamists see Islam not as a mere religion, but as a political ideology which should be integrated into all aspects of society (politics, law, economy, social justice, foreign policy, etc.). The traditional idea of Islam as an all-encompassing religion is extended to the complexity of a modern society. In fact they acknowledge the modernity of the society in terms of education, technology, changes in family structure, and so forth. The movement's founding fathers are Hassan Al Banna (1906–1949), Abul Ala Maududi, and, among the Shi'as, Baqer al Sadr, Ali Shariati and Ruhollah Khomeyni. They had a great impact among educated youth with a secular background, including women. They had less success among traditional ulamas [collective communities of Muslim religious and legal scholars]. To Islamists, the Islamic State should unite the ummah [Muslim people around the world] as much as possible, not being restricted to a specific nation. Such a state attempts to

recreate the golden age of the first decades of Islam and super-
sede tribal, ethnic and national divides, whose resilience is
attributed to the believers' abandonment of the true tenets of
Islam or to colonial policy. These movements are not necessarily
violent, even if, by definition, they are not democratic: the
Pakistani Jama'at Islami and the Turkish Refah Party as well as
most of the Muslim Brothers groups have remained inside a legal
framework, except where they were prevented from taking political action, as was the case in Syria, for instance.

The state the Islamist parties are challenging is not an
abstract state, but rather one that is more or less rooted in
history and is part of a strategic landscape. The Islamist
parties themselves are the product of a given political culture and society. Despite their claim of being supranational,
most of the Islamist movements have been shaped by
national particularities. Soon or later they tend to express
national interests, even under the pretext of Islamist ideology. A survey of the mainstream Islamist movements in the
1990s showed that they have failed in producing anything
resembling an "Islamist International," even if their ideological references remain similar.

This "nationalization" of Islamism is apparent in most
countries of the Middle East. Hamas challenges Arafat's PLO
not on points relating to Islam, but for "betraying" the
national interests of the Palestinian people. Turabi uses Islam
as a tool for unifying Sudan, by Islamizing the Southern
Christians and pagans. The Yemenite "Islah" movement has
been active in the re-unification of Yemen, against the wishes
of its Saudi Godfather. The Lebanese Hezbullah is now stressing the defense of the "Lebanese nation" and has established

a working relationship with many Christian circles. It has, incidentally, given up the idea of an Islamic State in Lebanon, due to consideration of the role of the Christians in defining the nation. The Turkish Refah Party, by stressing its Ottoman heritage, is trying to affirm a kind of neo-Ottoman Turkish model in the Middle East. By the same token, the Shi'i radical parties of Iraq, such as Dawa', are stressing the need for national unity and are closely working with non-Islamic national parties. The Algerian FIS claims to be the heir of the NLF of the anti-French war, and did not find roots in Morocco or Tunisia. During the Gulf War of 1991, each branch of the Muslim Brothers' organization took a stand in accordance with the perceived national interests of its own country (e.g., the Kuwait branch approved U.S. military intervention, while the Jordanian branch vehemently opposed it).

On the domestic scene, these parties brought previously excluded social strata into the political process: the mostazafin in Iran (the marginalized segments of the urban population); the Shi'as in Lebanon; recent city-dwellers and Kurds for the Refah; urban youth in Algeria, shocked by the bloody repression of October 1988; Northern tribes in Yemen, etc. In doing so they have helped to root nation-states and to create a domestic political scene, which is the only real basis for a future process of democratization. In this sense, the Islamist parties, while they are not democratic, foster the necessary conditions for an endogenous democracy, as is clearly the case in Iran. Khatami's election expressed a call for democracy which is possible only because the whole population has been brought into a common political scene by a popular and deep-rooted revolution.

Once this process is achieved, however, the mainstream Islamist movements, while consolidating a stable constituency inside their own country, are losing their appeal beyond their borders. The Refah (now Fazilet) has no influence abroad except in the Turkish migrant community in Western Europe, nor has the Islamic regime of Iran. This move let the road open for more radical movements which discard modern Nation-States and want to recreate the ummah, or the community of all Muslims in the world. Parallel to the growing Islamist political contest of the seventies and eighties, a process of conservative Islamization has been pervasive among the Muslim societies, which means, among other things, more veiled women in the streets and more shariat in state law. This Islamization is a consequence of deliberate state policy as well as a social phenomenon. Confronted with the Islamist opposition during the eighties, many Muslim states, even when officially secular, endeavored to promote a brand of conservative Islam and to organize an "official Islam." The first part of the program was quite a success, but state control has never been effective. In all these countries the impact of the development of a network of religious schools was the same: graduates holding a degree in religious sciences are now entering the labor market and tend, of course, to advocate the Islamization of education and law in order to get better job opportunities.

Three elements characterize these groups (well embodied by the Taliban/Osama bin Laden coalition). First, they combine political and militant jihad against the West with a very conservative definition of Islam, closer to the tenets of Saudi Wahhabism than to the official ideology of the Islamic

Republic of Iran. Nowhere is their conservatism more obvious than in their attitude toward women. While the Islamists strongly advocated women's education and political participation (with the condition of wearing a veil and attending single-sex schools), the neofundamentalists want to ban any female presence in public life. They are also strongly opposed to music, the arts, and entertainment. Contrary to the Islamists, they do not have an economic or social agenda. They are the heirs to the conservative Sunni tradition of fundamentalism, obsessed by the danger of a loss of purity within Islam through the influence of other religions. They stress the implementation of shariat as the sole criterion for an Islamic State and society. This strict Sunnism also turned very anti-Shi'a. This anti-Shi'a bias was revived at the end of the eighties as a consequence of the growing influence of the Saudi Wahhabism and gave way to a low-intensity civil war between Shi'as and Sunnis in Pakistan, reflected in Afghanistan by the mass killing of Shi'as after the take-over of Mazar-i Sharif by the Taliban in August 1998. But they also are becoming strongly anti-Christian and anti-Jewish. In fact, they believe that Israel, the U.S. and Iran are united to destroy "true Islam."

While anti-imperialist slogans were common among Islamist movements from the fifties on, and political anti-Zionism turned into anti-Semitism some time ago among many Muslim intellectual circles (and not necessarily religious), the anti-Christian propaganda among the new Sunni movements is rather new. The Islamists were not anti-Christians as such; in Iran during the revolution there has never been any attack on churches. The Egyptian Muslim Brothers never crack down on the Copts. The idea was that there is some common ground between true believers. Now, however, the term "religious war" really makes sense.

The second point is that these movements are supranational. A quick look at the bulk of bin Laden's militants killed or arrested between 1993 and 2001 show that they are mainly uprooted, western educated, having broken with their family as well as country of origin. They live in a global world. Of course the supranational links are sometimes made possible by infranational ones, like the common ethnic Pashtun background of the Taliban, the leader of the Pakistani Jama'at Islami (Qazi Husseyn), the head of one branch of the Jami'at Ulama (Senator Sami ul Haqq, from Akora Khattak), and many officers of the ISI (colonel Imad, adviser to the Taliban).

While Islamists do adapt to the nation-state, neo-fundamentalists embody the crisis of the nation-state, squeezed between infrastate solidarities and globalization. The state level is bypassed and ignored. The Taliban do not care about the state—they even downgraded Afghanistan by changing the official denomination from an "Islamic State" to an "Emirate." Mollah Omar does not care to attend the council of ministers, nor to go to the Capital.

In fact, this new brand of supranational neo-fundamentalism is more a product of contemporary globalization than of the Islamic past. Using two international languages (English and Arabic), traveling easily by air, studying, training and working in many different countries, communicating through the Internet and cellular phones, they think of themselves as "Muslims" and not as citizens of a specific country. They are often uprooted, more or less voluntarily (many are Palestinian refugees from 1948, and not from Gaza or the West Bank; bin Laden was stripped of his Saudi citizenship; many others belong to migrant families who move from one country to the next to find jobs or education). It is probably a paradox of globalization to gear together modern supranational networks and traditional, even archaic, infrastate forms of relationships (tribalism, for instance, or religious schools' networks). Even the very sectarian form of their religious beliefs and attitudes make the neo-fundamentalists look like other sects spreading all over the planet.

CHAPTER THREE

GLOBAL CONNECTIONS: CONFRONTATION

A professor of English and comparative literature at Columbia University for many years, Edward Said (1935–2003) was perhaps even better known as the world's foremost Palestinian intellectual and the most articulate champion of the rights of the Palestinian people. He was also a tireless explainer of the ways in which coverage of Islam and the Arab world by the media in the Western world was consistently tainted by preconceived notions, misconceptions, stereotypes, and outright bias.

The selection here is an excerpt from "Islam Through Western Eyes," Said's April 26, 1980, article in the Nation. *In it, Said expresses his concern that in the Western world, "the mere use of the term 'Islam' actually ends up becoming a form of attack, which in turn provokes more hostility between self-appointed Muslim and Western spokespersons." —JJ*

From "Islam Through Western Eyes"
by Edward Said
Nation, April 26, 1980

The media have become obsessed with something called "Islam," which in their voguish lexicon has acquired only two meanings, both of them unacceptable and impoverishing. On the one hand, "Islam" represents the threat of a resurgent atavism, which suggests not only the menace of a return to the Middle Ages but the destruction of what Senator Daniel Patrick Moynihan calls the democratic order in the Western world. On the other hand, "Islam" is made to stand for a defensive counterresponse to this first image of Islam as threat, especially when, for geopolitical reasons, "good" Moslems like the Saudi Arabians or the Afghan Moslem "freedom fighters" against the Soviet Union are in question. Anything said in defense of Islam is more or less forced into the apologetic form of a plea for Islam's humanism, its contributions to civilization, development and perhaps even to democratic niceness.

Along with that kind of counterresponse there is the occasional foolishness of trying to equate Islam with the immediate situation of one or another Islamic country, which in the case of Iran during the Shah's actual removal was perhaps a reasonable tactic. But after that exuberant period and during the hostage crisis, the tactic has become a somewhat trickier business. What is the Islamic apologist to say when confronted with the daily count of people executed by the Islamic komitehs, or when—as was reported on September 19, 1979, by Reuters—Ayatollah Ruhollah Khomeini announces that enemies of the Islamic revolution would be destroyed? The point is that both media meanings of "Islam" depend on each other, and are equally to be rejected for perpetuating the double bind . . .

From at least the end of the eighteenth century until our own day, modern Occidental reactions to Islam have been dominated by a type of thinking that may still be called Orientalist. The general basis of Orientalist thought is an imaginative geography dividing the word into two unequal parts, the larger and "different" one called the Orient, the other, also known as *our* world, called the Occident or the West. Such divisions always take place when one society or culture thinks about another one, different from it, but it is interesting that even when the Orient has uniformly been considered an inferior part of the world, it has always been endowed both with far greater size and with a greater potential for power than the West. Insofar as Islam has always been seen as belonging to the Orient, its particular fate within the general structure of Orientalism has been to be looked at with a very special hostility and fear. There are, of course, many obvious religious, psychological and political reasons for this, but all of these reasons derive from a sense that so far as the West is concerned, Islam represents not only a formidable competitor but also a late-coming challenge to Christianity.

I have not been able to discover any period in European or American history since the Middle Ages in which Islam was generally discussed or thought about *outside* a framework created by passion, prejudice and political interests. This may not seem like a surprising discovery, but included in the indictment is the entire gamut of scholarly and scientific disciplines which, since the early nineteenth century, have either called themselves Orientalism or tried systematically to deal with the Orient. No one would disagree with the statement that early commentators on Islam like Peter the Venerable and Barthelemy D'Herbelot were passionate Christian polemicists in what they they said. But it has been an unexamined assumption that since Europe advanced into the modern scientific age and freed itself of superstition and ignorance, the march must have included Orientalism.

Wasn't it true that Silvestre de Sacy, Edward Lane, Ernest Renan, Hamilton Gibb and Louis Massignon were learned, objective scholars, and isn't it true that, following upon all sorts of advances in twentieth-century sociology, anthropology, linguistics and history, American scholars who teach the Middle East and Islam in places like Princeton, Harvard and Chicago are therefore unbiased and free of special pleading in what they do? The answer is no. Not that Orientalism is more biased than other social and humanistic sciences; it is as ideological and as contaminated by the world as other disciplines. The main difference is that the Orientalists use the authority of their standing as experts to deny—no, to *cover*—their deep-seated feelings about Islam with a carpet of jargon whose purpose is to certify their "objectivity" and "scientific impartiality."

That is one point. The other distinguishes a historical pattern in what would otherwise be an undifferentiated characterization of Orientalism. Whenever in modern times there has been an acutely political tension felt between the Occident and its Orient (or between the West and its Islam), there has been a tendency to resort in the West not to direct violence but first to the cool, relatively detached instruments of scientific, quasi-objective representation. In this way Islam is made more clear, the true nature of its threat appears, an implicit course of action against it is proposed. In such a context both science and direct violence end up by being forms of aggression against Islam . . .

The Islamic Orient today is important for its resources or for its geopolitical location. Neither of these, however, is interchangeable with the interests, needs or aspirations of the native Orientals. Ever since the end of World War II, the

United States has been taking positions of dominance and hegemony once held in the Islamic world by Britain and France. With this replacement of one imperial system by another have gone two things: first, a remarkable burgeoning of academic and expert interest in Islam, and, second, an extraordinary revolution in the techniques available to the largely private-sector press and electronic journalism industries. Together these two phenomena, by which a huge apparatus of university, government and business experts study Islam and the Middle East and by which Islam has become a subject familiar to every consumer of news in the West, have almost entirely domesticated the Islamic world. Not only has that world become the subject of the most profound cultural and economic Western saturation in history—for no non-Western realm has been so dominated by the United States as the Arab-Islamic world is dominated today—by the exchange between Islam and the West, in this case the United States, is profoundly one-sided.

So far as the United States seems to be concerned, it is only a slight overstatement to say that Moslems and Arabs are essentially seen as either oil suppliers or potential terrorists. Very little of the detail, the human density, the passion of Arab-Moslem life has entered the awareness of even those people whose profession it is to report the Arab world. What we have instead is a series of crude, essentialized caricatures of the Islamic world presented in such a way as to make that world vulnerable to military aggression . . .

Even if military aggression does not occur, the implications of all this are far-reaching. As mentioned earlier, Islam has uniformly appeared to Europe and the West in general as a threat. Today, the phenomenon is more in evidence than ever before because on the one hand there has been an enormous media convergence upon what has been called the emergence, return or resurgence of Islam, and on the other hand, because parts of the Islamic world—Palestine, Iran, Afghanistan, among other places—which have been undergoing various unequal processes of historical development, have also seemed to be encroaching upon traditional Western (more particularly *American*) hegemony. The views of the experts and of the media are nearly identical on this. Far from attempting to refine, or even dissent from, the gross image of Islam as a threat, the intellectual and policy community in the United States has considerably enforced and concentrated the image. From Zbigniew Brzezinski's vision of the "crescent of crisis" to Bernard Lewis's "return of Islam," the picture drawn is a unanimous one. "Islam" means the end of civilization as "we" know it. Islam is anti-human, antidemocratic, anti-Semitic, antirational. University scholars whose professional lives are tied to the study of Islam have either been willing collaborators with this state of things, or if they have been silent, their marginality in the culture at large further confirms the fact that in the United States at least, there is no major segment of the polity, no significant sector of the culture, no part of the whole community capable of identifying sympathetically with the Islamic world.

On the other hand, most of the Third World is now fully bathed in U.S.-produced TV shows, and is wholly dependent upon a tiny group of news agencies that transmit news back to the Third World, even in the large numbers of cases where the news is *about* the Third World. From being the source of news, the Third World generally, and Islamic countries in particular, have become consumers of news. For the first time in history (for the first time, that is, on such a scale) the Islamic world may be said to be learning *about itself* in part by means of images, histories and information manufactured in the West. If one adds to this fact that students and scholars in the Islamic world are still dependent upon U.S. and European libraries and institutions of learning for what now passes as Middle Eastern studies (consider, for example, that there isn't a single first-rate, usable library of Arabic material in the entire Islamic world), plus the fact that English is a world language in a way that Arabic isn't, plus the fact that for its elite the Islamic world is now producing a managerial class of basically subordinate natives who are indebted for their economies, their defense establishments and for their political ideas to the worldwide consumer-market system controlled in the West—one gets an accurate, although extremely depressing, picture of what the media revolution (serving a small segment of the societies that produced it) has done to Islam.

To the extent that Islam is known about today, it is known principally in the form given it by the mass media: not only radio, films and TV but also textbooks, magazines and best-selling, high-quality novels. This corporate picture of Islam on the whole is a depressing and misleading one. What emerges is that Ayatollah Khomeini, Col. Muammar e-Qaddafi, Sheik Ahmad Zaki Yamani and Palestinian terrorists are the best-known figures in the foreground, while the background is populated by shadowy (though extremely frightening) notions about *jihad*, slavery, subordination of women and irrational violence combined with extreme licentiousness. If you were to ask an average literate Westerner to name an Arab or Islamic writer, or a musician, or an intellectual, you might get a name like Kahlil Gibran in response, but nothing else. In other words, whole swatches of Islamic history, culture and society simply do not exist except in the truncated, tightly packaged forms made current by the media. As Herbert Schiller has said, TV's images tend to present reality in too immediate and fragmentary a form for either historical or human continuity to appear. Islam therefore is equivalent to an undifferentiated mob of scimitar-waving oil suppliers, or it is reduced to the utterances of one or another Islamic leader who at the moment happens to be a convenient foreign scapegoat.

———■———

If the West, and particularly the United States, needed a wake-up call concerning the galvanizing political potential of Islamist movements in their societies, it came with the Iranian Revolution of the late 1970s, which overthrew Iran's ruling monarch, Shah Mohammad Reza Pahlavi, and replaced him with an Islamic government headed by the Shiite Muslim cleric Ayatollah Ruholla Mussaui Khomeini (1902–1989). For decades under the shah, Iran had been the United States' most important ally in the Middle East, and the success of the Islamist revolution there caught U.S. policymakers by surprise.

The Iranian government installed by Khomeini and his fellow mullahs (clergy members) remains in power in Iran today. In this sense, the Iranian

Revolution has served as an inspiration to many of today's Islamist movements, particularly in its vehemently anti-American rhetoric. Among other things, Khomeini famously referred to the United States as the "Great Satan," and his followers were fond of proclaiming "Death to America!"

The section below is from Khomeini's best-known work, Hukumat-i-Islami *(Islamic Government). —JJ*

From *Islamic Government*
by Ayatollah Ruholla Khomeini
1970

This slogan of the separation of religion and politics and the demand that Islamic scholars not intervene in social and political affairs have been formulated and propagated by the imperialists; it is only the irreligious who repeat them. Were religion and politics separate in the time of the Prophet (peace and blessings be upon him)! Did there exist, on one side, a group of clerics, and opposite it, a group of politicians and leaders? Were religion and politics separate in the time of the caliphs—even if they were not legitimate—or in the time of the Commander of the Faithful (upon whom be peace)! Did two separate authorities exist? These slogans and claims have been advanced by the imperialists and their political agents in order to prevent religion from ordering the affairs of this world and shaping Muslim society, and at the same time to create a rift between the scholars of Islam, on the one hand, and the masses and those struggling for freedom and independence, on the other. They have thus been able to gain dominance over our people and plunder our resources, for such has always been their ultimate goal . . .

If you pay no attention to the policies of the imperialists, and consider Islam to be simply the few topics you are always studying and never go beyond them, then the imperialists will leave you alone. Pray as much as you like; it is your oil they are after—why should they worry about your prayers! They are after our minerals, and want to turn our country into a market for their goods. That is the reason the puppet governments they have installed prevent us from industrializing, and instead, establish only assembly plants and industry that is dependent on the outside world.

They do not want us to be true human beings, for they are afraid of true human beings. Even if only one true human being appears, they fear him, because others will follow him and he will have an impact that can destroy the whole foundation of tyranny, imperialism, and government by puppets. So whenever some true human being has appeared, they have either killed him or imprisoned and exiled him, and tried to defame him by saying: "This is a political akhund!" Now the Prophet (peace and blessings be upon him) was also a political person. This evil propaganda is undertaken by the political agents of imperialism only to make you shun politics, to prevent you from intervening in the affairs of society and struggling against treacherous governments and their anti-national and anti-Islamic policies. They want to work their will as they please, with no one to bar their way. . .

A body of laws alone is not sufficient for a society to be reformed. In order for law to ensure the reform and happiness of man, there must be an executive power and an executor. For this reason, God Almighty, in addition to revealing a body of law (i.e., the ordinances of the shari'a), has laid down a particular form of government together with executive and administrative institutions.

The Most Noble Messenger (peace and blessings be upon him) headed the executive and administrative institutions of Muslim society. In addition to conveying the revelation and expounding and interpreting the articles of faith and the ordinances and institutions of Islam, he undertook the implementation of law and the establishment of the ordinances of Islam, thereby bringing into being the Islamic state. He did not content himself with the promulgation of law; rather, he implemented it at the same time, cutting off hands and administering lashings and stonings. After the Most Noble Messenger, his successor had the same duty and function. When the Prophet appointed a successor, it was not for the purpose of expounding articles of faith and law; it was for the implementation of law and the execution of God's ordinances.

It was this function—the execution of law and the establishment of Islamic institutions—that made the appointment of a successor such an important matter that the Prophet would have failed to fulfill his mission if he had neglected it. For after the Prophet, the Muslims still needed someone to execute laws and establish the institutions of Islam in society, so that they might attain happiness in this world and the hereafter.

By their very nature, in fact, law and social institutions require the existence of an executor. It has always and everywhere been the case that legislation alone has little benefit: legislation by itself cannot assure the well-being of man. After the establishment of legislation, an executive power must come into being, a power that implements the laws and the verdicts given by the courts, thus allowing people to benefit from the laws and the just sentences the courts deliver. Islam has therefore established an executive people in the same way that it has brought laws into being. The person who holds this executive power is known as the valiamr.

The path of the Prophet constitutes a proof of the necessity for establishing government. First, he himself established a government, as history testifies. He engaged in the implementation of laws, the establishment of the ordinances of Islam, and the administration of society. He sent out governors to different regions; both sat in judgment himself and appointed judges; dispatched emissaries to foreign states, tribal chieftains, and kings; concluded treaties and pacts; and took command in battle. In short, he fulfilled all the functions of government. Second, he designated a ruler to succeed him, in accordance with divine command. If God Almighty, through the Prophet, designated a man who was to rule over Muslim society after him, this is in itself an indication that government remains a necessity after the departure of the Prophet from this world. Again, since the Most Noble Messenger promulgated the divine command through his act of appointing a successor, he also implicitly stated the necessity for establishing a government.

It is self-evident that the necessity for enactment of the law, which necessitated the formation of a government by the Prophet (upon whom be peace), was not confined or restricted to his time, but continues after his departure from this world. According to one of the noble verses of the Qur'an, the ordinances of Islam are not limited with respect to time or place; they are permanent and must be enacted until the end of time. They were not revealed merely for the time of the Prophet, only to be abandoned thereafter, with retribution and the penal code of Islam no longer to be enacted, or the taxes prescribed by Islam no longer collected, and the defense of the lands and people of Islam suspended. The claim that the laws of Islam may remain in abeyance or are restricted to a particular time or place is contrary to the essential credal bases of Islam. Since the enactment of laws, then, is necessary after the departure of the Prophet from this world, and indeed, will remain so until the end of time, the formation of a government and the establishment of executive and administrative organs are also necessary. Without the formation of a government and the establishment of such organs to ensure that through enactment of the law, all activities of the individual take place in the framework of a just system, chaos and anarchy will prevail and social, intellectual, and moral corruption will arise. The only way to prevent the emergence of anarchy and disorder and to protect society from corruption is to form a government and thus impart order to all the affairs of the country.

———□———

Inspired by events in Iran, Afghan Islamists began to rebel against the government in their own country in 1979. The government had been installed by the Soviet Union and still relied on Soviet support for its survival. In December 1979, the Soviet Union invaded Afghanistan to end the unrest there. The Islamist resistance only intensified, however, in the form of armed opposition by guerrilla fighters known as mujahideen, which literally means "participants in jihad" and is most often translated as "holy warriors."

Having been surprised by recent events in Iran, the United States now saw an opportunity to strike at the

*Soviet Union, its Cold War rival, by supporting the
mujahideen. Working through its sometime ally, the
neighboring Muslim nation of Pakistan, the United
States financed, armed, and equipped the mujahideen
for ten years, until the Soviet forces finally withdrew in
1989. During this time, the mujahideen became a sacred
cause in the Muslim world, and Islamists from many
different nations journeyed to Afghanistan. Among them
was a wealthy young Saudi Arabian by the name of
Osama bin Laden. In the 1990s, bin Laden became the
protégé of the Taliban, the extremely strict Islamic fundamentalist group that ultimately took power in
Afghanistan after the Soviets left. Below are three separate sets of decrees imposed by the Taliban after it took
power, indicating the severity of its interpretation of
Islam. The atrocious syntax and grammar of the
English translation below are apparently intended to
convey the execrable quality of the Taliban's grasp of
Dari (an Afghan language) in the original. Many
Taliban officials were barely literate in anything but the
Koran, much of which they committed to memory
through oral repetition. —JJ*

Decrees by the Taliban
November 1996

Decree announced by the General Presidency of Amr Bil Maruf
and Nai Az Munkar (Religious Police.)

Women you should not step outside your residence. If you
go outside the house you should not be like women who used

to go with fashionable clothes wearing much cosmetics and appearing in front of every men before the coming of Islam.

Islam as a rescuing religion has determined specific dignity for women, Islam has valuable instructions for women. Women should not create such opportunity to attract the attention of useless people who will not look at them with a good eye. Women have the responsibility as a teacher or co-ordinator for her family. Husband, brother, father have the responsibility for providing the family with the necessary life requirements (food, clothes etc).

In case women are required to go outside the residence for the purposes of education, social needs or social services they should cover themselves in accordance with Islamic *Sharia* regulation. If women are going outside with fashionable, ornamental, tight and charming clothes to show themselves, they will be cursed by the Islamic *Sharia* and should never expect to go to heaven.

All family elders and every Muslim have responsibility in this respect. We request all family elders to keep tight control over their families and avoid these social problems. Otherwise these women will be threatened, investigated and severely punished as well as the family elders by the forces of the Religious Police (Munkrat).

The Religious Police (Munkrat) have the responsibility and duty to struggle against these social problems and will continue their effort until evil is finished.

Kabul, November 1996

Rules of work for the State Hospitals and private clinics based on Islamic *Sharia* principles. Ministry of Health, on behalf of *Amir ul Momineen Mullah* Mohammed Omar.

1. Female patients should go to female physicians. In case a male physician is needed, the female patient should be accompanied by her close relative.
2. During examination, the female patients and male physicians both should be dressed with Islamic *hijab* (veil).
3. Male physicians should not touch or see the other parts of female patients except for the affected part.
4. Waiting room for female patients should be safely covered.
5. The person who regulates turn for female patients should be a female.
6. During the night duty, in what rooms which female patients are hospitalized, the male doctor without the call of the patient is not allowed to enter the room.
7. Sitting and speaking between male and female doctors are not allowed, if there be need for discussion, it should be done with *hijab*.
8. Female doctors should wear simple clothes, they are not allowed to wear stylish clothes or use cosmetics or make-up.
9. Female doctors and nurses are not allowed to enter the rooms where male patients are hospitalized.
10. Hospital staff should pray in mosques on time.
11. The Religious Police are allowed to go for control at any time and nobody can prevent them.

Anybody who violates the order will be punished as per Islamic regulations.

Kabul, December 1996

General Presidency of Amr Bil Maruf

1. To prevent sedition and female uncovers (Be Hejabi). No drivers are allowed to pick up women who are using

Iranian burqa. In case of violation the driver will be imprisoned. If such kind of female are observed in the street their house will be found and their husband punished. If the women use stimulating and attractive cloth and there is no accompany of close male relative with them, the drivers should not pick them up.

2. To prevent music. To be broadcasted by the public information resources. In shops, hotels, vehicles and rickshaws cassettes and music are prohibited. This matter should be monitored within five days. If any music cassette found in a shop, the shopkeeper should be imprisoned and the shop locked. If five people guarantee the shop should be opened the criminal released later. If cassette found in the vehicle, the vehicle and the driver will be imprisoned. If five people guarantee the vehicle will be released and the criminal released later.

3. To prevent beard shaving and its cutting. After one and a half months if anyone observed who has shaved and/or cut his beard, they should be arrested and imprisoned until their beard gets bushy.

4. To prevent keeping pigeons and playing with birds. Within ten days this habit/hobby should stop. After ten days this should be monitored and the pigeons and any other playing birds should be killed.

5. To prevent kite-flying. The kite shops in the city should be abolished.

6. To prevent idolatory. In vehicles, shops, hotels, room and any other place pictures/ portraits should be abolished. The monitors should tear up all pictures in the above places.

7. To prevent gambling. In collaboration with the security police the main centers should be found and the gamblers imprisoned for one month.

8. To eradicate the use or addiction. Addicts should be imprisoned and investigation made to find the supplier and the shop. The shop should be locked and the owner and user should be imprisoned and punished.

9. To prevent the British and American hairstyle. People with long hair should be arrested and taken to the Religious Police department to shave their hair. The criminal has to pay the barber.

10. To prevent interest on loans, charge on changing small denomination notes and charge on money orders. All money exchangers should be informed that the above three types of exchanging the money should be prohibited. In case of violation criminals will be imprisoned for a long time.

11. To prevent washing cloth by young ladies along the water streams in the city. Violator ladies should be picked up with respectful Islamic manner, taken to their houses and their husbands severely punished.

12. To prevent music and dances in wedding parties. In the case of violation the head of the family will be arrested and punished.

13. To prevent the playing of music drum. The prohibition of this should be announced. If anybody does this then the religious elders can decide about it.

14. To prevent sewing ladies cloth and taking female body measures by tailor. If women or fashion magazines are seen in the shop the tailor should be imprisoned.

15. To prevent sorcery. All the related books should be burnt and the magician should be imprisoned until his repentance.

16. To prevent not praying and order gathering pray at the bazaar. Prayer should be done on their due times in all districts. Transportation should be strictly prohibited and all people are obliged to go to the mosque. If young people are seen in the shops they will be immediately imprisoned.

———————■———————

Among the so-called Afghan Arabs who flocked to Pakistan and Afghanistan in the 1980s for the jihad was Abdullah Azzam (1941–1989). A Palestinian by birth, Azzam introduced the Islamic principle of jihad to the Palestinian opposition to Israel by helping to establish Hamas, which has since supplanted the Palestine Liberation Organization (PLO) as Israel's most implacable enemy as well as the resistance group that most appeals to Palestinian youth. While financing and advising the mujahideen in Afghanistan, Azzam also served as a mentor to Osama bin Laden, whom he had first met while teaching Islamic law at a university in Saudi Arabia. (Another one of Bin Laden's professors there was Mohammad Qutb, the exiled brother of Sayyid al-Qutb.) His life, which is further outlined in the biographical sketch on the next page, illustrates the sophisticated international nature of the modern Islamist movement as well as the complex interconnections between events in the Islamic world. —JJ

"Abdullah Azzam: The Godfather of Jihad"
by Chris Suellentrop
Slate.com, April 16, 2002

As the Lenin of international jihad, Abdullah Azzam didn't invent his movement's ideas, but he furthered them and put them into practice around the world. He constructed the religious ideology for the war against the Soviets in Afghanistan, recruited Arab mujahideen to implement his vision, and built the international network that his disciple, Osama Bin Laden, would turn into al-Qaida. Azzam applied his ideas in his native Palestine, too, where he served as a founding member of Hamas. After Sept. 11, Americans believed that Bin Laden transformed the world in one swift stroke. But it was Azzam who, years before, laid the groundwork for the current wars in Afghanistan and the Middle East.

Political Islam's Great Communicator and traveling salesman, Azzam trotted the globe during the 1980s to promote the Afghan jihad against the Soviets. By the time of his death in 1989, he had recruited between 16,000 and 20,000 mujahideen from 20 countries to Afghanistan, visited 50 American cities to advance his cause, and dispatched acolytes to spread the gospel in 26 U.S. states, not to mention across the Middle East and Europe. His Mujahideen Services Bureau in Peshawar, Pakistan, served as a way station and training ground for fresh recruits as they arrived. Among those inspired by Azzam: Mohammed Salameh, convicted of conspiracy, assault, and explosives charges for his involvement in the 1993 World Trade Center bombing; Wadih El-Hage and

Mohammed Odeh, convicted for their roles in the 1998 East African embassy bombings; and Osama Bin Laden. The *Encyclopedia of the Afghan Jihad*, an 11-volume al-Qaida training manual, names two men in its dedication. One is Bin Laden, who is listed as the "faithful helper" of the other man, Abdullah Azzam.

Why should we care about Azzam now, 13 years after his death? Because his ideas live on after him, fueling the conflagrations in Afghanistan and Palestine. Azzam proclaimed that any land that was once ruled by the Islamic caliphate, even if it were as small as the span of a person's hand, must be recaptured if it falls into the hands of infidels. As he wrote in *Defense of Muslim Lands*, his best-known booklet, "With reference to the Russians, it is not permitted to negotiate with them until they retreat from every hand span of Muslim territory. With the Jews in Palestine, likewise." This doctrine roused Bin Laden to issue his 1998 fatwa declaring that Muslims must kill Americans in order to expel the United States from Saudi Arabia's holy sites. It also sheds light on the "tragedy of Andalusia," a phrase mentioned on the Oct. 7 videotape released by Bin Laden and his lieutenants. If the caliphate is to be restored to its full glory, radical Muslims must reconquer all of Islam's historic lands, including southern Spain.

The caliphate also included, of course, Palestine, by which Azzam meant Israel. Unlike Bin Laden, who was (is?) more concerned with toppling secular Arab regimes, Azzam insisted that the Palestinian cause was pre-eminent. As a young man, Azzam fought in the Six Day's War, fleeing to Jordan after Israel occupied his hometown, a West Bank village near Jenin. In 1970, he broke with Yasser Arafat's

Palestine Liberation Organization because he believed the PLO was too secular. He accused the PLO of trying to overthrow Jordan's King Hussein rather than focusing on the true goal, the destruction of Israel.

Azzam's dispute with the PLO foreshadowed a disagreement that developed between him and Bin Laden in the late 1980s. As the battle with the Russians approached endgame, Bin Laden hoped to wage jihad on multiple fronts, simultaneously against the United States and against the profane rulers of the many nations from which the mujahideen had been recruited. Azzam, however, had always seen the Afghan war as a training ground for the ultimate war in Palestine. Now he hoped to transfer the mujahideen to his homeland and take the war directly to Israel.

Already, Azzam had helped to establish Hamas, and during the first intifada in 1987, Arafat's PLO was forced to co-opt Azzam's ideas and rhetoric when Hamas championed them. (Yossef Bodansky, in *Bin Laden: The Man Who Declared War on America*, says the PLO also sent Palestinian youths to Afghanistan for mujahideen training.) Azzam had redefined the conflict: For many, Palestinians were no longer engaged in a nationalist struggle to establish a state. They were conducting an uncompromising battle to reclaim lost Muslim lands. "There will be no solution to the Palestinian problem except through jihad," Azzam wrote in accordance with his motto, "Jihad and the rifle alone: no negotiations, no conferences, no dialogues."

Before he could attempt to carry out his plans, Azzam was assassinated in Peshawar by a car bomb. (His murder was never solved, though the Pakistani Interservices Intelligence Agency, the CIA, and Bin Laden have all been touted as suspects.) Bin

Laden assumed control of Azzam's organization and directed it toward his ends. Azzam's hopes of a climactic struggle with Israel appeared dashed.

More than a decade later, however, Azzam's vision appears triumphant. The Arab mujahideen never followed him home to Palestine, but his ideas took root there. The result is delivering suicide bombers into the heart of Israel, fulfilling the dream he expressed during a 1988 speech: "The Palestinian youth came here to Afghanistan, and also non-Palestinians, and they were trained, and their souls became prepared, and the paranoia of fear disappeared, and they became experts. Now, every one of them returns . . . ready to die."

CHAPTER FOUR

POWER, AUTHORITY, AND GOVERNMENT: JIHAD

In the recent era of conflict between Islam and the Western world, the concept of jihad, or holy war, has been much discussed. Although the Koran clearly allows, and even exhorts, faithful Muslims to "fight" against the enemies of Islam, interpreters differ widely as to what jihad legitimately entails. For some, jihad represents nothing more than the daily struggle to live the righteous life of a Muslim in a largely godless world. Indeed, many Muslims, if not most, interpret jihad as meaning something closer to "struggle for the faith" rather than literal "holy war." For others, jihad authorizes defensive war against those who would oppress Muslims or oppose Islam. Still others interpret this defensive aspect of jihad much more broadly, asserting that jihad permits violent action against all those who fail to actively embrace Islam. Extreme Islamist groups from the Muslim Brotherhood to Hezbollah, Hamas, and Al Qaeda have used the concept of jihad as a rationale for their actions.

The first selection on the next page is from one of Islam's prominent early commentators on the Koran. Taqi ad-Din Ahmad ibn Taymiyah (1263–1328) lived and taught in the important Muslim cities of Cairo,

Baghdad, and Damascus. His call for a strict literal interpretation of the Koran, without any polytheistic moderations, was a great influence on the work of Muhammad ibn Abdul-Wahhab and continues to profoundly influence today's Islamist groups. In the selection below, he explains why it is necessary for the faithful to commit themselves to jihad. —JJ

From "The Religious and Moral Doctrine of Jihad"
by Taqi ad-Din Ahmad ibn Taymiyah
Fourteenth Century

That then is the jihad against the unbelievers (kufaar), the enemies of Allah and His Messenger. For whoever has heard the summons of the Messenger of Allah, and has not responded to it, must be fought, "until there is no persecution and the religion is Allah's entirely." [Qur'an, 2:193, 8:39]

When Allah sent His Prophet and ordered him to summon the people to His religion, He did not permit him to kill or fight anyone for that reason before the Prophet emigrated to Medina . . .

Then, after that, He imposed fighting on them with the following words:

Prescribed for you is fighting, though it be hateful to you. Yet it may happen that you will hate a thing which is better for you; and it may happen that you love a thing which is worse for you. Allah knows and you know not. [Qur'an, 2:216]

. . . There are numerous similar verses in the Qur'an and equally frequent is the glorification of jihad and those who participate in it:

O believers, shall I direct you to a commerce that shall deliver you from a painful chastisement? You shall believe in Allah and His Messenger, and struggle in the way of Allah with your possessions and your selves. That is better for you, did you but know. He will forgive you your sins and admit you into gardens underneath which rivers flow, and to dwelling places goodly in Gardens of Eden; that is the mighty triumph; and other things you love, help from Allah and a nigh victory. Give thou good tidings to the believers. [Qur'an, 61:10–13]

And [elsewhere] He has said:

Do you reckon the giving of water to pilgrims and the inhabiting of the Holy Masjid as the same as one who believes in Allah and the Last Day and struggles in the way of Allah? Not equal are they in Allah's sight; and Allah guides not the people of the evildoers. Those who believe, and have emigrated, and have struggled in the way of Allah with their possessions and their selves are mightier in rank with Allah; and those—they are the triumphant; their Lord gives them good tidings of mercy from Him and good pleasure; for them await gardens wherein is lasting bliss, therein to dwell forever and ever; surely with Allah is a mighty wage. [Qur'an, 9:19–21]

. . . The command to participate in jihad and the mention of its merits occur innumerable times in the Qur'an and the Sunnah.

Therefore it is the best voluntary (religious) act that man can perform. All scholars agree that it is *better* than the *hajj* (greater pilgrimage) and the *'umrah* (lesser pilgrimage), than voluntary salaat and voluntary fasting, as the Qur'an and the Sunnah indicate.

The Prophet has said:

The head of the affair is Islam, its central pillar is the salaat and the summit is the jihad.

And he has said:

In Paradise there are a hundred grades with intervals as wide as the distance between the sky and the earth. All these Allah has prepared for those who take part in jihad.

There is unanimity about the authenticity of this Tradition:

A day and a night spent in ribaat (remaining at the frontiers of Islam with the intention of defending Islamic territory against the enemies) are better than one month spent in fasting and vigils. If he dies (in the fulfillment of this task), he will receive the recompense of his deeds and subsistence, and he will be protected from the Angel of the Grave.

It is related in the Sunan that:

A day spent in ribaat in the way of Allah is better than a thousand days spent elsewhere.

He has said,

Two eyes will not be touched by the fire: the eye that has wept out of fear for Allah, and the eye that has spent the night on the watch in the way of Allah.

. . . This is a vast subject, unequalled by other subjects as far as the reward and merit of human deeds is concerned. This is evident upon closer examination. The [first] reason is that the benefit of jihad is general, extending not only to the person who participates in it but also to others, both in a religious and a temporal sense.

[Secondly,] jihad implies all kinds of worship, both in its inner and outer forms. More than any other act it implies love and devotion for Allah, Who is exalted, trust in Him, the surrender of one's life and property to Him, patience, asceticism, remembrance of Allah and all kinds of other acts [of worship]. And the individual or community that participates in it, finds itself between two blissful outcomes: either victory and triumph or martyrdom and Paradise.

[Thirdly,] all creatures must live and die. Now, it is in jihad that one can live and die in ultimate happiness, both in this world and in the Hereafter. Abandoning it means losing entirely or partially both kinds of happiness. There are people who want to perform religious and temporal deeds full of hardship in spite of their lack of benefit, whereas actually jihad is religiously and temporally more beneficial than any other deed full of hardship. Other people [participate in it] out of a desire to make things easy for themselves when death meets them, for the death of a martyr is easier than any other form of death. In fact, it is the best of all manners of dying.

Since lawful warfare is essentially jihad and since its aim is that the religion is Allah's entirely [2:189, 8:39] and Allah's word is uppermost [9:40], therefore, according to all Muslims, those who stand in the way of this aim must be fought . . .

———■———

This selection illustrates the concept of jihad taken to its most militant extreme by the most radical Islamist groups. It is the notorious February 23, 1998, fatwa issued by Osama bin Laden and four other leaders of extremist Islamist groups calling for "every Muslim" to engage in a jihad to "kill the Americans and plunder their money wherever and whenever they find it." Note the specific American foreign policy practices objected to in the document and that it refers to Americans as crusaders—a reference to the European attacks on the Middle East during the Middle Ages.

A fatwa is a ruling on Islamic law issued by a recognized Islamic religious authority. It should be noted that few Muslims would recognize the religious authority of bin Laden to pronounce a fatwa and that most Muslims would regard the pronouncements here as unacceptably extreme. The document also refers to the Muslim ulema, which is the body of wise men trained in Islamic law and history and thereby recognized as having authority to issue opinions and judgments about such things. —JJ

"Jihad Against Jews and Crusaders"
by Osama bin Laden, Ayman al-Zawahiri, Abu-Yasir Rifa'i Ahmad Taha, Mir Hamzah, and Fazlur Rahman
February 23, 1998

Praise be to Allah, who revealed the Book, controls the clouds, defeats factionalism, and says in His Book: "But when the forbidden months are past, then fight and slay the pagans wherever ye find them, seize them, beleaguer them, and lie in wait for them in every stratagem (of war)"; and peace be upon our Prophet, Muhammad Bin-'Abdallah, who said: "I have been sent with the sword between my hands to ensure that no one but Allah is worshipped, Allah who put my livelihood under the shadow of my spear and who inflicts humiliation and scorn on those who disobey my orders."

The Arabian Peninsula has never—since Allah made it flat, created its desert, and encircled it with seas—been stormed by any forces like the crusader armies spreading in it like locusts, eating its riches and wiping out its plantations. All this is happening at a time in which nations are attacking Muslims like people fighting over a plate of food. In the light of the grave situation and the lack of support, we and you are obliged to discuss current events, and we should all agree on how to settle the matter.

No one argues today about three facts that are known to everyone; we will list them, in order to remind everyone:

First, for over seven years the United States has been occupying the lands of Islam in the holiest of places, the Arabian Peninsula, plundering its riches, dictating to its rulers, humiliating its people, terrorizing its neighbors, and turning its bases in the Peninsula into a spearhead through which to fight the neighboring Muslim peoples.

If some people have in the past argued about the fact of the occupation, all the people of the Peninsula have now acknowledged it. The best proof of this is the Americans' continuing aggression against the Iraqi people using the Peninsula as a staging post, even though all its rulers are against their territories being used to that end, but they are helpless.

Second, despite the great devastation inflicted on the Iraqi people by the crusader-Zionist alliance, and despite the huge number of those killed, which has exceeded 1 million . . . despite all this, the Americans are once against trying to repeat the horrific massacres, as though they are not content with the protracted blockade imposed after the ferocious war or the fragmentation and devastation.

So here they come to annihilate what is left of this people and to humiliate their Muslim neighbors.

Third, if the Americans' aims behind these wars are religious and economic, the aim is also to serve the Jews' petty state and divert attention from its occupation of Jerusalem and murder of Muslims there. The best proof of this is their eagerness to destroy Iraq, the strongest neighboring Arab state, and their endeavor to fragment all the states of the region such as Iraq, Saudi Arabia, Egypt, and Sudan into paper statelets and through their disunion and weakness to guarantee Israel's survival and the continuation of the brutal crusade occupation of the Peninsula.

All these crimes and sins committed by the Americans are a clear declaration of war on Allah, his messenger, and

Muslims. And ulema have throughout Islamic history unanimously agreed that the jihad is an individual duty if the enemy destroys the Muslim countries. This was revealed by Imam Bin-Qadamah in "Al-Mughni," Imam al-Kisa'i in "Al-Bada'i," al-Qurtubi in his interpretation, and the shaykh of al-Islam in his books, where he said: "As for the fighting to repulse [an enemy], it is aimed at defending sanctity and religion, and it is a duty as agreed [by the ulema]. Nothing is more sacred than belief except repulsing an enemy who is attacking religion and life."

On that basis, and in compliance with Allah's order, we issue the following fatwa to all Muslims:

> *The ruling to kill the Americans and their allies—civilians and military—is an individual duty for every Muslim who can do it in any country in which it is possible to do it, in order to liberate the al-Aqsa Mosque and the holy mosque [Mecca] from their grip, and in order for their armies to move out of all the lands of Islam, defeated and unable to threaten any Muslim. This is in accordance with the words of Almighty Allah, "and fight the pagans all together as they fight you all together," and "fight them until there is no more tumult or oppression, and there prevail justice and faith in Allah."*

This is in addition to the words of Almighty Allah: "And why should ye not fight in the cause of Allah and of those who, being weak, are ill-treated (and oppressed)?—women and children, whose cry is: 'Our Lord, rescue us from this town, whose people are oppressors; and raise for us from thee one who will help!'"

We—with Allah's help—call on every Muslim who believes in Allah and wishes to be rewarded to comply with

Allah's order to kill the Americans and plunder their money wherever and whenever they find it. We also call on Muslim ulema, leaders, youths, and soldiers to launch the raid on Satan's U.S. troops and the devil's supporters allying with them, and to displace those who are behind them so that they may learn a lesson.

Almighty Allah said: "O ye who believe, give your response to Allah and His Apostle, when He calleth you to that which will give you life. And know that Allah cometh between a man and his heart, and that it is He to whom ye shall all be gathered."

Almighty Allah also says: "O ye who believe, what is the matter with you, that when ye are asked to go forth in the cause of Allah, ye cling so heavily to the earth! Do ye prefer the life of this world to the hereafter? But little is the comfort of this life, as compared with the hereafter. Unless ye go forth, He will punish you with a grievous penalty, and put others in your place; but Him ye would not harm in the least. For Allah hath power over all things."

Almighty Allah also says: "So lose no heart, nor fall into despair. For ye must gain mastery if ye are true in faith."

Born in Egypt in 1951, Ayman al-Zawahiri was trained as a physician. A member of the Muslim Brotherhood and the leader of Egyptian Jihad, another radical Islamist group, al-Zawahiri traveled to Afghanistan to join the mujahideen in the 1980s. It was here that he first met and joined forces with

*Osama bin Laden. Today, al-Zawahiri is generally
described as bin Laden's right-hand man and chief
strategist in Al Qaeda. The selection below is
excerpted from a longer manuscript by al-Zawahiri,
discovered in Afghanistan by U.S. troops and entitled
"Knights Under the Prophet's Banner." It was apparently intended by al-Zawahiri to serve as his "last will
and testament" in the event of his death and illustrates
the scope and dimension of the jihad as conceived by
al-Zawahiri and Al Qaeda. —JJ*

From "Knights Under the Prophet's Banner"
by Ayman al-Zawahiri
December 2001

The jihad movement must come closer to the masses, defend
their honor, fend off injustice, and lead them to the path of
guidance and victory. It must step forward in the arena of sacrifice and excel to get its message across in a way that makes
the right accessible to all seekers and that makes access to the
origin and facts of religion simple and free of the complexities
of terminology and the intricacies of composition.

The jihad movement must dedicate one of its wings to
work with the masses, preach, provide services for the Muslim
people, and share their concerns through all available avenues
for charity and educational work. We must not leave a single
area unoccupied. We must win the people's confidence, respect,
and affection. The people will not love us unless they felt that
we love them, care about them, and are ready to defend them.

In short, in waging the battle the jihad movement must be in the middle, or ahead, of the nation. It must be extremely careful not to get isolated from its nation or engage the government in the battle of the elite against the authority.

We must not blame the nation for not responding or not living up to the task. Instead, we must blame ourselves for failing to deliver the message, show compassion, and sacrifice.

The jihad movement must be eager to make room for the Muslim nation to participate with it in the jihad for the sake of empowerment [al-tamkin]. The Muslim nation will not participate with it unless the slogans of the mujahidin are understood by the masses of the Muslim nation.

The one slogan that has been well understood by the nation and to which it has been responding for the past 50 years is the call for the jihad against Israel. In addition to this slogan, the nation in this decade is geared against the US presence. It has responded favorably to the call for the jihad against the Americans.

A single look at the history of the mujahidin in Afghanistan, Palestine, and Chechnya will show that the jihad movement has moved to the center of the leadership of the nation when it adopted the slogan of liberating the nation from its external enemies and when it portrayed it as a battle of Islam against infidelity and infidels.

The strange thing is that secularists, who brought disasters to the Muslim nation, particularly on the arena of the Arab-Israeli conflict; and who started the march of treason by recognizing Israel beginning with the Armistice Agreement of 1949, as we explained earlier, are the ones who talk the most about the issue of Palestine.

Stranger still is the fact that the Muslims, who have sacrificed the most for Jerusalem, whose doctrine and Shari'ah prevent them from abandoning any part of Palestine or recognizing Israel, as we explained earlier; and who are the most capable of leading the nation in its jihad against Israel are the least active in championing the issue of Palestine and raising its slogans among the masses.

The jihad movement's opportunity to lead the nation toward jihad to liberate Palestine is now doubled. All the secular currents that paid lip service to the issue of Palestine and competed with the Islamic movement to lead the nation in this regard are now exposed before the Muslim nation following their recognition of Israel's existence and adoption of negotiations and compliance with the international resolutions to liberate what is left, or permitted by Israel, of Palestine. These currents differ among themselves on the amount of crumbs thrown by Israel to the Muslim and the Arabs.

The fact that must be acknowledged is that the issue of Palestine is the cause that has been firing up the feelings of the Muslim nation from Morocco to Indonesia for the past 50 years. In addition, it is a rallying point for all the Arabs, be they believers or non-believers, good or evil . . .

Through this jihad the stances of the rulers, their henchmen of ulema of the sultan [reference to pro-government clerics], writers, and judges, and the security agencies will be exposed. By so doing, the Islamic movement will prove their treason before the masses of the Muslim nation and demonstrate that the reason for their treason is a flaw in their faith. They have allied themselves with the enemies of God against

His supporters and antagonized the mujahidin, because of their Islam and jihad, in favor of the Jewish and Christian enemies of the nation. They have committed a violation of monotheism by supporting the infidels against the Muslims.

Tracking down the Americans and the Jews is not impossible. Killing them with a single bullet, a stab, or a device made up of a popular mix of explosives or hitting them with an iron rod is not impossible. Burning down their property with Molotov Cocktails is not difficult. With the available means, small groups could prove to be a frightening horror for the Americans and the Jews . . .

Armies achieve victory only when the infantry takes hold of land. Likewise, the mujahid Islamic movement will not triumph against the world coalition unless it possesses a fundamentalist base in the heart of the Islamic world. All the means and plans that we have reviewed for mobilizing the nation will remain up in the air without a tangible gain or benefit unless they lead to the establishment of the state of caliphate in the heart of the Islamic world.

Nur-al-Din Zanki, and Salah-al-Din al-Ayyubi [Saladin] after him, may God bless their souls, have fought scores of battles until Nur-al-Din managed to wrestle Damascus from of the hands of the hypocrites and unified Greater Syria under his command. He sent Salah-al-Din to Egypt, where he fought one battle after another until he brought Egypt under his control. When Egypt and Syria were unified after the death of Nur-al-Din, the mujahid Sultan Salah-al-Din managed to win the battle of Hittin and conquered Bayt al-Maqdis [Islamic name for Jerusalem]. Only then did the cycle of history turn against the Crusaders.

If the successful operations against Islam's enemies and the severe damage inflicted on them do not serve the ultimate goal of establishing the Muslim nation in the heart of the Islamic world, they will be nothing more than disturbing acts, regardless of their magnitude, that could be absorbed and endured, even if after some time and with some losses.

The establishment of a Muslim state in the heart of the Islamic world is not an easy goal or an objective that is close at hand. But it constitutes the hope of the Muslim nation to reinstate its fallen caliphate and regain its lost glory . . .

Liberating the Muslim nation, confronting the enemies of Islam, and launching jihad against them require a Muslim authority, established on a Muslim land, that raises the banner of jihad and rallies the Muslims around it. Without achieving this goal our actions will mean nothing more than mere and repeated disturbances that will not lead to the aspired goal, which is the restoration of the caliphate and the dismissal of the invaders from the land of Islam.

This goal must remain the basic objective of the Islamic jihad movement, regardless of the sacrifices and the time involved.

―――――■―――――

For many observers, one of the most frightening and unfathomable tactics of the militant Islamist extremists is the use of so-called suicide bombers. In the conflict between Islam and the West, suicide bombers first came to prominence as the hallmark of Hamas, the Palestinian resistance group, although they have since become even more commonplace, as in the Iraq War, for example.

The selection below is an excerpt from a 1999 U.S. government report on profiling terrorists. Later published in book form as Who Becomes a Terrorist and Why: The 1999 Government Report on Profiling Terrorists, *the report was written by Rex Hudson and the staff of the Federal Research Division of the Library of Congress. The specific excerpt below is from the section of the report dealing with the motivations of suicide bombers. —JJ*

From *Who Becomes a Terrorist and Why: The 1999 Government Report on Profiling Terrorists*
by Rex Hudson and the Staff of the Federal Research Division of the Library of Congress
1999

The other of the two approaches that have predominated, the terrorist as fanatic, emphasizes the terrorist's rational qualities and views the terrorist as a cool, logical planning individual whose rewards are ideological and political, rather than financial. This approach takes into account that terrorists are often well educated and capable of sophisticated, albeit highly biased, rhetoric and political analysis.

Notwithstanding the religious origins of the word, the term "fanaticism" in modern usage, has broadened out of the religious context to refer to more generally held extreme beliefs. The terrorist is often labeled as a fanatic, especially in actions that lead to self-destruction. Although fanaticism is not unique to terrorism, it is, like "terrorism," a pejorative term. In psychological terms, the concept of fanaticism carries some implications of mental illness, but, Taylor (1988:97) points out, it "is not a diagnostic category in mental illness." Thus, he believes that "Commonly held assumptions about the relationship between fanaticism and mental illness . . . seem to be inappropriate." The fanatic often seems to view the world from a particular perspective lying at the extreme of a continuum.

Two related processes, Taylor points out, are prejudice and authoritarianism, with which fanaticism has a number of cognitive processes in common, such as an unwillingness to compromise, a disdain for other alternative views, the tendency to see things in black-and-white, a rigidity of belief, and a perception of the world that reflects a closed mind. Understanding the nature of fanaticism, he explains, requires recognizing the role of the cultural (religious and social) context. Fanaticism, in Taylor's view, may indeed " . . . be part of the cluster of attributes of the terrorist." However, Taylor emphasizes that the particular cultural context in which the terrorist is operating needs to be taken into account in understanding whether the term might be appropriate.

Suicide Terrorists

Deliberate self-destruction, when the terrorist's death is necessary in order to detonate a bomb or avoid capture, is not a common feature of terrorism in most countries, although it happens occasionally with Islamic fundamentalist terrorists in the Middle East and Tamil terrorists in Sri Lanka and southern

India. It is also a feature of North Korean terrorism. The two North Korean agents who blew up Korean Air Flight 858 on November 28, 1987, popped cyanide capsules when confronted by police investigators. Only one of the terrorists succeeded in killing himself, however. Prior to mid-1985, there were 11 suicide attacks against international targets in the Middle East using vehicle bombs. Three well-known cases were the bombing of the U.S. Embassy in Beirut on April 18, 1983, which killed 63 people, and the separate bombings of the U.S. Marine barracks and the French military headquarters in Lebanon on October 23, 1983, which killed 241 U.S. Marines and 58 French paratroopers, respectively. The first instance, however, was the bombing of Israel's military headquarters in Tyre, in which 141 people were killed. Inspired by these suicide attacks in Lebanon and his closer ties with Iran and Hizballah, Abu Nidal launched "suicide squads" in his attacks against the Rome and Vienna airports in late December 1985, in which an escape route was not planned.

The world leaders in terrorist suicide attacks are not the Islamic fundamentalists, but the Tamils of Sri Lanka. The LTTE's track record for suicide attacks is unrivaled. Its suicide commandos have blown up the prime ministers of two countries (India and Sri Lanka), celebrities, at least one naval battleship, and have regularly used suicide to avoid capture as well as simply a means of protest. LTTE terrorists do not dare not to carry out their irrevocable orders to use their cyanide capsules if captured. No fewer than 35 LTTE operatives committed suicide to simply avoid being questioned by investigators in the wake of the Gandhi assassination. Attempting to be circumspect, investigators disguised themselves as doctors in order to question LTTE patients undergoing medical treatment, but, Vijay Karan (1997:46) writes about the LTTE patients, "Their reflexes indoctrinated to react even to the slightest suspicion, all of them instantly popped cyanide capsules." Two were saved only because the investigators forcibly removed the capsules from their mouths, but one investigator suffered a severe bite wound on his hand and had to be hospitalized for some time.

To Western observers, the acts of suicide terrorism by adherents of Islam and Hinduism may be attributable to fanaticism or mental illness or both. From the perspective of the Islamic movement, however, such acts of self-destruction have a cultural and religious context, the historical origins of which can be seen in the behavior of religious sects associated with the Shi'ite movement, notably the Assassins (see *Glossary*). Similarly, the suicide campaign of the Islamic Resistance Movement (Hamas) in the 1993-94 period involved young Palestinian terrorists, who, acting on individual initiative, attacked Israelis in crowded places, using home-made improvised weapons such as knives and axes. Such attacks were suicidal because escape was not part of the attacker's plan. These attacks were, at least in part, motivated by revenge.

According to scholars of Muslim culture, so-called suicide bombings, however, are seen by Islamists and Tamils alike as instances of martyrdom, and should be understood as such. The Arabic term used is istishad, a religious term meaning to give one's life in the name of Allah, as opposed to intihar, which refers to suicide resulting from personal distress. The latter form of suicide is not condoned in Islamic teachings.

There is a clear correlation between suicide attacks and concurrent events and developments in the Middle Eastern area.

For example, suicide attacks increased in frequency after the October 1990 clashes between Israeli security forces and Muslim worshipers on Temple Mount, in the Old City of Jerusalem, in which 18 Muslims were killed. The suicide attacks carried out by Hamas in Afula and Hadera in April 1994 coincided with the talks that preceded the signing by Israel and the PLO of the Cairo agreement. They were also claimed to revenge the massacre of 39 and the wounding of 200 Muslim worshipers in a Hebron mosque by an Israeli settler on February 25, 1994. Attacks perpetrated in Ramat-Gan and in Jerusalem in July and August 1995, respectively, coincided with the discussions concerning the conduct of elections in the Territories, which were concluded in the Oslo II agreement. The primary reason for Hamas's suicide attacks was that they exacted a heavy price in Israeli casualties. Most of the suicide attackers came from the Gaza Strip. Most were bachelors aged 18 to 25, with high school education, and some with university education. Hamas or Islamic Jihad operatives sent the attackers on their missions believing they would enter eternal Paradise.

Glossary

ASSASSINS—From the eleventh through the thirteenth century, a sect of Shiite Muslims called the Assassins used assassination as a tool for purifying the Muslim religion. The Assassins' victims, who were generally officials, were killed in public to communicate the error of the targeted official. By carrying out the assassination in public, the Assassin would allow himself to be apprehended and killed in order to demonstrate the purity of his motives and to enter Heaven.

References

Karan, Vijay. *War by Stealth: Terrorism in India*. New Delhi, India: Viking (Penguin Books India), 1997.

Taylor, Maxwell, and Helen Ryan. "Fanaticism, Political Suicide and Terrorism," *Terrorism*, 11, No. 2, 1988, 91-111.

CHAPTER FIVE

CIVIC IDEAS AND PRACTICE: ISLAM IN EUROPE

In many ways, today's Europe is a crucial location for the story of Islam and the West. Muslims in Europe today are the largest immigrant group on the continent. That presence has forced Europeans to reexamine their attitudes regarding immigrants, Muslims, and the role of religious faith in secular, democratic societies. Similarly, the presence of Muslims in Europe as a minority in a secular society has made those Muslims reconsider many of their own attitudes. The following selection was originally published in Time *magazine's European edition and provides a useful introductory overview of this issue. —JJ*

"Islam in Europe: A Changing Faith"
by Nicholas Le Quesne
Time Europe, December 24, 2001

There's standing room only in a converted warehouse in the decaying industrial hinterland north of central Paris. It's mid-October, just days after the first U.S. bombs fell on Afghanistan, and the French magazine *La Médina*—which

serves as an outlet for the country's Muslim population—
has organized a public meeting on the significance for Islam
of the Sept. 11 attacks and their aftermath.

The atmosphere is electric. The men are in jeans and
sportswear, while most of the women wear scarves over their
heads. With few exceptions, the audience is made up of North
Africans in their mid-20s. On the podium, 39-year-old Swiss
university professor Tariq Ramadan—whose grandfather
founded Egypt's Islamic revival movement the Muslim
Brotherhood in 1928—begins to speak. "Now more than ever
we need to criticize some of our brothers," he tells the packed
hall. "My dignity depends on saying, 'You're unjustified if you
use the Koran to justify murder.'" The French establishment—
with its traditional mistrust of religion—views Ramadan with
suspicion, but tonight he sounds like the voice of reason.

Then a young woman steps up to the microphone. With
her black *hijab* she could be from almost anywhere in the
Muslim world, but her accent is unmistakable—it's pure northern Parisian: "It's urgent for Muslims today to do everything
they can to make the truth about their religion understood."
The crowd bursts into thunderous applause.

Although most media have focused on a hard-core fringe
calling for armed struggle against America, the overwhelming
majority of Europe's Muslims see their religion as a moderate
one. A survey carried out by the Mori agency for Eastern Eye,
Britain's biggest selling Asian newspaper, shows that 87% of
the Muslims polled are loyal to Britain, even though 64%
oppose the U.S.-led strikes against Afghanistan.

These people and thousands of others like them are
crafting a new strand of Islam, one that aims to reconcile the

basic tenets of the faith—such as social justice and submission to the will of God—with the realities of contemporary European life. Though this process has been under way for some time, the events of Sept. 11 and afterward have lent it new urgency.

For many of Europe's 12.5 million Muslims, now is the time to redefine Islam in the context of their identities as believers who were born and bred in Europe. The result is a kind of Euro-Islam, the traditional Koran-based religion with its prohibitions against alcohol and interest-bearing loans now indelibly marked by the "Western" values of tolerance, democracy and civil liberties. This new vision could well end up influencing the world these young Europeans' grandparents left behind.

For this new generation, Euro-Islam is not a zero sum game: it is possible to be Muslim and European at the same time. In fact, unlike that of their Christian neighbors, the religious faith of Europe's Muslims is getting stronger. A survey published by French newspaper *Le Monde* in October shows that people from Muslim backgrounds are praying more, attending mosques more often and observing the Ramadan fast more assiduously than they did in 1994, when the survey was last conducted. The increased devotion is particularly marked among those who have been to university. In Britain, more women are wearing the *hijab* today than 10 years ago.

Euro-Islam is a bridge between two cultures, providing young believers with a way of respecting inherited traditions while living in a different world. It also gives them the confidence to practice their religion more openly, unlike their parents or grandparents who thought their sojourn in Europe was temporary and so were content to express their faith in private. Their children view Europe as their home and see no reason not to worship more publicly.

During *Ramadan*, the holy month of fasting that ended last week, Ahmid—a Moroccan-born imam at an Islamic cultural center in Rome—was selling Korans and cassettes of Muslim preachers at his stall outside the central mosque. A practicing Muslim back in Morocco, Ahmid has become more devout since arriving in Italy 13 years ago. "The immigrant turns to religion for support," he says. "Muslims have always gone anywhere in the world and adapted to learn to live as they must—and let others live their lives."

As Ahmid suggests, the story of Islam in Europe is a story of immigration. During the Continent's reconstruction after World War II, Britain and France turned to their former colonies in South Asia and North Africa to fill their manpower shortages, while Germany opened its doors to "guest workers" from Turkey. Most of these guests never went home again, and their children were born and grew up as Europeans. Today, the Muslim communities in these three countries are the biggest in Europe: 5 million in France, 3.2 million in Germany and 2 million in Britain. These numbers have been augmented by more recent waves of immigration to countries like Spain, the Netherlands, Italy, Belgium and the Scandinavian region.

But Islam itself is nothing new in Europe. After advancing as far as Tours in 732, the Arabs remained in Spain until 1492, when they were driven from Granada. Over those centuries they bequeathed the Spanish their distinctive pronunciation of the letter J as well as masterpieces of

Moorish architecture. The Islamic scholars Ibn Sina and Ibn
Rushd reintroduced Greek philosophy to the West during the
Middle Ages, while Arab mathematicians revolutionized science with the invention of algebra. And when the Ottoman
armies pushed west through the Balkan peninsula in the 14th
century, they established Muslim communities in Central
Europe that still exist today.

In Sarajevo, the imams' calls to prayer from recon-
structed mosques blend with the chimes of bells from
Orthodox Christian medieval churches and 19th century cathe-
drals. "I have more in common with Bosnian Serbs than
Muslims from Pakistan and Afghanistan," says former Bosnian
Interior Minister Muhamad Besic. His words offer striking testimony of the strength of Islam's historic roots on the
Continent, given that not 10 years ago his city was under siege
from those same Bosnian Serbs. But they also speak of an
assimilation that even war could not affect.

What's different now is that for the first time in their
14-century history, Muslims are living as minorities in secular societies. Traditional Islamic theology divides the world
into two zones: the *dar al-Islam*, or house of Islam, and the
dar al-harb, or house of war. This world view assumes that
Muslims will never be able to practice their religion properly
in non-Muslim lands and so should not settle there. But sec-
ond- and third-generation Muslims in Europe quickly
discovered that this was a false opposition. Fresh ideas were
needed, such as the *dar ash-shahada*, or house of testimony: a
new concept referring to any place where Muslims can make
their profession of faith and live according to the precepts
of their religion.

Tariq Ramadan is one of the most prominent exponents of this new thinking. "As a Muslim I can be at home anywhere I'm safe and where the rule of law protects my freedom of conscience and my freedom to worship," he says. "In this new environment, my responsibility is to bear witness to the message of my faith."

European Muslims don't necessarily differ from other Muslims when it comes to the basic tenets of that faith, but according to Dilwar Hussain, a research fellow at the Islamic Foundation in Leicester, they do have "greater flexibility, greater awareness of the wider society and more liberal attitudes." Witness the growing number of Muslim girls contacting the Rutgers Women's Health Foundation in the Netherlands for abortion advice.

Hussain says that Europe's liberal attitudes are forcing the faithful to reassess their own beliefs. "The younger Muslims are going back to the text and asking: 'What my parents used to do, is that really part of my faith or is that part of their cultural tradition?' Drawing that distinction between faith and culture is very important. You may find some things in the Islamic texts, and then the cultural setting can lead to a particular interpretation. When the cultural setting changes, those interpretations will naturally change." Says Lhaj Thami Breze, president of the Union of Islamic Organizations of France: "We're forging our own way of practicing Islam, and it's going to be different from the way it's done in Morocco, Algeria or Saudi Arabia. Islam needs to free itself from imported customs."

For Yakob Mahi, 36, a Moroccan imam living in Belgium, adapting Islam to new environments has been central to the development of his faith. He cites the concept of *Shari'a*, the way of life ordained by God for mankind, which he says many countries have turned into a code of punishment—even though less than 1% of the Koran consists of penal rules. In Europe, Mahi says, "We can see *Shari'a* not as law, but as a path to be understood in its context. When we transform it into daily European life, we see that *Shari'a* doesn't mean cutting off the hand of a thief. Rather it's a spirit present in many things we enjoy in Europe: the principles of democracy, the rule of law, the freedoms of expression and association." That innovative interpretation makes Muslim law compatible with its Western secular counterparts. So Mahi advocates a doctrine of "spiritual citizenship" in which Muslims "respect the laws [of the secular state] but try to give a spiritual impulse to everything they do."

In Europe, Muslims must also confront social questions—such as euthanasia, abortion and sexuality—that are suppressed in many Islamic countries. Nowhere is this confrontation more obvious than in the assertive roles being claimed by women. After all, the 7th century doctrines of the Prophet Muhammad considerably improved their lot, forbidding the then common practice of female infanticide and making the education of girls a sacred duty. "It's not the religion that holds back women but the culture—and the men," says Fatma Amer, head of education and interfaith relations at the London Central Mosque. "It's up to the women to organize themselves and not accept everything their communities tell them they must do."

One area in which both women and men are asserting themselves more vigorously is marriage. In Britain, increasing numbers of young women are resisting arranged marriages to cousins back in Bangladesh or Pakistan. In France, too, young people are clashing with parents who always assumed their children would marry someone from their own village in Morocco or Algeria. "We want to choose the person we marry," says Fouad Imarraine, who runs the Tawhid Cultural Center in the Paris suburb of Saint-Denis. "It doesn't matter what color their skin is as long as we're of the same faith."

Imarraine describes how the attitudes of Europe's Muslims have changed. "When we went back to North Africa on holiday, we realized we had deeper ties in France," he says, sipping coffee in a café nestled at the foot of concrete tower blocks. "Very few of my generation made it to university and Islam provided us with a refuge from failure at school and feeling shut out of society. But there's now a younger generation using Islam as a way of establishing the universal values they have in common with those around them. Defining their own identity as Muslims is a way of interacting with the rest of society."

This generation has grown up thinking of Europe as home, even if it has often seemed inhospitable. Schoolgirls have been expelled for wearing the *hijab* in France, while in British Islamic communities like the one in Luton, Muslims are twice as likely to be unemployed as other townsfolk. But for this new generation, being Muslim and European means their faith has become a matter of individual choice rather than social constraint.

"Younger Muslims are far more individualistic in the way they interpret the Koran, but that doesn't necessarily mean they're any less devout," says Mustapha Oukbih, a 36-year-old journalist who lives and works in the Hague. The Dutch website Maghreb.nl, for example, has hosted chat rooms to discuss whether it's okay for Muslim newlyweds to have oral sex. "They want to decide for themselves how to live their lives," Oukbih says. This emphasis on personal choice is providing many Muslims with a new vision of politics, too.

"Strictly religious problems are becoming more marginal," says Hakim El Ghissassi, editor of France's *La Médina*, referring to the widespread availability of mosques and religious instruction. "Young people today are more concerned with resolving the social issues facing Muslims: employment, equality in the labor market, political representation and the way that history is taught in schools. Muslims are going to make their voices heard more and more on these issues. They're going to want to take part in government at the local, national and European level."

For the moment, though, Muslim political representation is small. With a Muslim population of 800,000, the Netherlands has seven Muslim M.P.s. Britain has only two, and France none. Yet people like Bassam Tibi, a professor of international relations at the University of Göttingen who coined the term Euro-Islam, insist that the integration of Europe's Muslims depends on the adoption of a form of Islam that embraces Western political values, such as pluralism, tolerance, the separation of church and state, democratic civil society and individual human rights. "The options for Muslims are unequivocal," says Tibi. "There is no middle way between Euro-Islam and a ghettoization of Muslim minorities."

In Britain, that view is shared by the writer and critic Ziauddin Sardar, who came to the country with his Pakistani parents as a child in the 1960s. "If there is a sociological change there will be a theological change as well," he says. "In Islam, law and ethics are the same thing. If you change the ethics, you change the law. There will be a new interpretation of Islam."

This new interpretation is taking shape in different places at different speeds. Although non-Muslims often view Islam as a monolithic bloc, the religion is characterized by its diversity. With over a billion believers scattered across every continent, as well as separate Shi'ite and Sunni traditions, the Muslim community (or *ummah*) has long been a philosophical construct rather than a demographic reality. That's true in Europe, where Muslims are divided by country of residence as much as by country of origin. "The problems Muslims are facing here are deeply influenced by the institutions of the countries where they live," says Farhad Khosrokhavar, a professor at Paris' School of Post-Graduate Studies in Social Science. "But the influence of democracy and religious tolerance is bringing about a meeting of minds."

And that influence could well spread to the Muslim world as a whole. For Zaki Badawi, chairman of the Imams and Mosques Council of Britain, Muslims in the West are helping to answer the question that has haunted Islam for the past century: how to reconcile tradition and modernity. "Islam, like any other society, finds modernity challenging," Badawi says. Although that challenge is felt more acutely in the developing world, intellectuals in those countries don't have the freedom to analyze the problem and find effective solutions. "The tension between Islam and modernity will be answered by thinkers in the West," Badawi says, "and transferred back to our native countries."

It would be symbolically and historically fitting if the next great reform of Islam came from the *diaspora* in the West. After all, the starting point of the Muslim calendar is not the year of Muhammad's birth but the day 1,379 years ago when the Prophet led his followers from his birthplace in Mecca to found a new community in Medina. "The very foundation of Islamic civilization was built on diaspora, on the move from Mecca to Medina," says British Muslim writer Sardar. "This is where the *diaspora* is very important: in creating a truly moderate tradition for the future." The new *diaspora* of Muslims in Europe already has that task in hand.

One way in which Western and Islamic societies greatly differ is in their attitudes toward relations between the sexes. Islamic practices generally call for a segregation of men and women, with women maintaining what can only be regarded as a subservient position to men. The sexual freedom of Muslim women, in everything from dating to marriage, is drastically restricted by Western standards. These restrictions extend to clothing, with Muslim beliefs generally calling for women to dress with a severe modesty. In practice, this calls for Muslim women to cover most of their bodies, especially their heads.

In France, which has a large Muslim immigrant population, these beliefs have recently led to a controversial law banning head scarves in public schools. Public life in France celebrates the principles of "liberty, equality, and fraternity," the proud legacy of the French Revolution at the end of the eighteenth century. Among the ways the French apply such principles is by eliminating any intrusion of religion into public life, including in public education. For the French, the wearing of head scarves in school violates this principle and threatens the freedom and equality of Muslim immigrants by hindering their full assimilation into French society.

The article below is by one of the government officials responsible for the law on head scarves and explains the reasoning behind it. —JJ

"A Nation in Diversity: France, Muslims and the Headscarf"
by Patrick Weil
OpenDemocracy.net, March 25, 2004

On 3 July 2003, President Jacques Chirac of France established an independent commission to study the implementation of the principle of *laïcité* (secularism) in the French republic.

In the previous weeks, the issue of violence in public schools had risen to a level of visibility so high in the media and the public eye that the French national assembly had already created a special commission run by its president to study the issue of "religious symbols in schools." The presidential commission had a wider scope—*laïcité* in the whole society. Its composition was also more open: its nineteen members consisted of school principals and teachers, academics, civil servants, businesspeople and parliamentarians—a group also with very diverse origins, religious beliefs and political opinions.

I was a member of this presidential commission, most likely chosen for my expertise in the field of immigration policy and nationality law, and as a former member of the high advisory council on integration. I arrived with the idea that a law was probably unnecessary for resolving the problems. Yet, after four months of public hearings involving representatives of all religious confessions, political parties, trades unions and NGOs, as well as individual actors—principals, teachers, parents, students, directors of hospitals and jails, company managers—I endorsed a report recommending twenty-five different measures, including the banning of conspicuous religious symbols in public schools. I would like here to explain why.

But let me emphasise one point at the start, before setting out the background and reasoning of my decision. After we heard the evidence, we concluded that we faced a difficult choice with respect to young Muslim girls wearing the headscarf in state schools. Either we left the situation as it was, and thus supported a situation that denied freedom of choice to those—the very large majority—who do not want to wear the headscarf; or we endorsed a law that removed freedom of choice from those who do want to wear it.

We decided to give freedom of choice to the former during the time they were in school, while the latter retain all their freedom for their life outside school.

But in any case—and this is the fact I want to emphasise at the start—complete freedom of choice for all was, unfortunately, not on offer. This was less a choice between freedom and restriction than a choice between freedoms; our commission was responsible for advising on how such freedoms should both be guaranteed and limited in the best interests of all.

Testimonies of Faith, Voices of Freedom

The French tradition of *laïcité* was built against the influence, indeed domination, of the Catholic Church in public affairs. The 1905 law of separation between the church and the state was a victory for the majority of French citizens educated in Catholic faith, but who wanted the Catholic Church to be excluded from public education and influence.

Yet this was not anti-religious legislation. The 1905 law also recognised the right of everyone to practice his or her own beliefs, to the point where the state even paid the salaries of religious officials in order to allow those obliged to live in confined institutions (asylums, prisons, the army, residential schools, hospitals) to practice their faith.

The law did not forbid the wearing of religious signs, but the custom in France was (and still is) to keep religious faith as a private matter. This tradition is most likely linked in France to the long battle against the power and public exposure of Catholic faith: in the relation between the individual, the religious group and the state, the latter is both expected and seen to act as protector of the individual against group pressure.

But our commission did not base its proposals on this custom, nor on a human right that emerged in the half-century after 1905, the equality of women and men. Either approach would have meant an intrusive interpretation of a religious symbol which, clearly, can have different meanings in different circumstances.

Whereas for a majority of women the headscarf is an expression of the domination of women by men (a view strongly expressed by many women refugees from Iran), it can also be the articulation of a free belief; a means of protection against the pressure of males; an expression of identity and freedom against secular parents; a statement of opposition to western and secular society.

The state has no right to "adjudicate" between these meanings, or to interpret religious symbols *tout court*. After all, if the headscarf had been banned (for example) on the basis of discrimination against women, it would have been necessary to do so not only in schools, but across the whole of society.

Moreover, France since 1905 has formally acceded to international rules and conventions of various kinds—most recently the European Union, the European Convention on Human Rights, and many other international conventions that recognise the individual's right publicly to express religious belief. It was on this basis that in 1989 the French *Conseil d'Etat* (supreme court) stated that the Muslim headscarf is not in itself an ostentatious symbol that could be banned from schools; it could only be forbidden if it were used as an instrument of pressure on girls who were reluctant to wear it.

What, then, has changed since 1989? In this period, and especially in the last two to three years, it has become clear that in schools where some Muslim girls do wear the headscarf and others do not, there is strong pressure on the latter to "conform". This daily pressure takes different forms, from insults to violence. In the view of the (mostly male) aggressors, these girls are "bad Muslims", "whores", who should follow the example of their sisters who respect Koranic prescriptions.

We received testimonies of Muslim fathers who had to transfer their daughters from public to (Catholic) private schools where they were free of pressure to wear the headscarf. Furthermore, in the increasing number of schools where girls wear the *hijab*, a clear majority of Muslim girls who do not wear the headscarf called for legal protection and asked the commission to ban all public displays of religious belief.

A large majority of Muslim girls do not want to wear the scarf; they too have the right of freedom of conscience. Principals and teachers have tried their best to bring back some order in an impossible situation where pressure, insults or violence sets pupils against one another, yet where to protest against this treatment is seen as treason to the community. There are cases where pupils who have had their arms broken in violent acts have lied to their parents in order to avoid denouncing their peers.

A Complex Emotional Territory

We on the presidential commission studied many possible solutions. I myself considered making a distinction between school courtyards and the classroom itself, and enforcing rules concerning a dress code only in the latter. Another possibility was to devolve authority over religious symbols to school principals at a local level.

But after four months of inquiries and hearings, our commission did not endorse such solutions. Rather, our near-unanimous sentiment (there was one dissident among our group of nineteen) was that we had to understand and then address the issue at a national level rather than merely a local one.

The reason was plain: the wearing of a headscarf or the imposition of it on others is much more than an issue of individual freedom: it has become a France-wide strategy pursued by fundamentalist groups who use public schools as their battleground. A devolution of decisions to local level would guarantee permanent tension between principals and these groups who would have relentlessly targeted individual schools in order to attract, week by week, public and press attention.

This lay behind our proposal to ban conspicuous signs of religious adherence (including Jewish skullcaps and large crucifixes). We did this in full awareness and respect of the European Convention of Human Rights, which authorises limiting expressions of religious faith in circumstances where these create problems of public order or attacks on the freedom of conscience of others.

The ban concerns only public schools because there, those concerned are minors. There is no question of forbidding religious display in universities or elsewhere in the adult world. Adults have means of defence that children do not; they can go to court and otherwise claim their right of freedom of conscience in ways children cannot.

We made this choice after long reflection and hesitation, both individual and collective, but with a valid expectation that the majority of Muslim families in France would endorse it or at least be relieved.

A minority of Muslims in France are anti-religious; a small minority is fundamentalist and consider that *sharia* (Islamic) law is superior to civic law; a large majority do not want to impose the headscarf on their daughters but are also discomfited by any suggestion of infidelity to their religious tradition.

It is members of this third group, hitherto vulnerable to pressure from friends, neighbours or family members who want to impose the headscarf on their daughters, who can now reply:

"I was ready to follow your advice, but now it is impossible: I cannot disobey the law! "

The space of feeling opened up here is reminiscent of that shared by many Algerian immigrants when their children born in France were automatically granted French nationality. Abdelmalek Sayad describes this well in his book *The Suffering of the Immigrant* (Polity, 2004). Algerians could never have applied for this individually, he writes, but they were discreetly satisfied when it was "imposed" by law:

> *The beneficiaries of [French] nationality, acquired without having applied for it, adapt to their situation well, and protestations of circumstance (which can be perfectly sincere in other respects) cannot convince to the contrary. Their circle, who would not have accepted an act of naturalisation that followed an ordinary process, later appear relieved that French nationality . . . occurred by itself, as a constraint collectively imposed: it is a condition shared by all, not the result of individual and voluntary acts where some called attention to themselves and separated themselves from the others. . . Despite protestations of all sorts that are the "right thing" to proclaim, despite the guilt or simple unease that continues to be felt by the naturalised, this "forced" naturalisation finally produces something like a satisfaction which, for a whole series of reasons, asks to remain secret and, sometimes, resigned to.*

Making History Anew

The emotional logic is clear: a ban on religious display via the law, from the "outside", ensures the protection of children from fundamentalist pressure yet does not enforce a break in religious ties.

I admit that the law passed by the French parliament has one unfortunate consequence: the right of Muslim girls who freely want to wear the scarf in public schools, without pressuring anyone else, is denied. What will happen to them if, after the period of dialogue established by the law, they do not want to remove their scarf? It is most likely that they will be offered the opportunity to attend private religious schools—probably Catholic, Protestant or Jewish (there are only three Muslim schools in France). These schools, if they are under state contract (as 95% are), have an obligation to accept applications from pupils of other faiths.

More Muslim schools under state contract (which entails authority over the curriculum) will develop in future. The French state historically gives large subsidies to this "parallel" educational sector, enabling the tuition fees to remain very inexpensive. The Muslim community, like other faiths, has the right to establish schools where the customs and holidays of its faith are observed, and where religious instruction exists alongside the national curriculum.

But my single, strong regret as a result of this commission process does not relate to the headscarf issue as such: it is that the ban on religious signs in public schools is the only one of our twenty-five proposals yet implemented by President Chirac, his government, and the national assembly.

Certainly, religious fundamentalism needs to be fought and contained when it challenges the basic values of democracy. It also has its own autonomous dynamic and is not the simple product of social injustice. But our commission also recommended stringent policies to address the social factors favouring the rise of fundamentalist influence. France has not done enough to correct the ethnic, racial, and religious discriminations that negatively affect most children of North African immigrants. School history lessons do not acknowledge slavery or colonisation as a full part of our national history.

There is also an urgent need to adapt to the new diversity of the French religious landscape in order to sustain one of the main principles of *laïcité*: equality of all faiths before the law. France has the largest Buddhist, Jewish and Muslim communities of any European country; but the scale and currency of the Muslim presence in France makes a focus on it more necessary.

Thus, for example, our commission demanded that the French state respect fully the freedom to build mosques, and observe funerary rituals and culinary customs. We even proposed that the most important religious feasts of minority faiths be recognised as public holidays, to mark the respect of the entire French community towards their compatriots. This last proposal was rejected by the government and coolly received by most socialist leaders, but 40% of citizens immediately supported it and it provoked a very intense, fruitful and creative debate in millions of families across France. I am certain that it will return to the public agenda.

The historical success of the French model of secularisation, *laïcité*, rests on its guarantee to individuals of state protection against pressure from any religious group. But its future success requires a flexible capacity to respect cultural and religious diversity—and to consider this diversity not a burden, but a challenge and an opportunity.

As has happened in other societies that have found them-selves hosts to large groups of immigrants, the democracies of Europe have not always welcomed the newcomers in their midst. In recent years, France, Belgium, the Netherlands, and Germany, all of which are now homes to sizable Muslim immigrant populations, have experienced a right-wing backlash against immi-grants and the rise of anti-immigrant political parties. In most cases, the specific targets of the anti-immigrant backlash are Muslims. The article below is from the New York Times *and describes the rise of the anti-Muslim right-wing movement in Belgium.* —JJ

"Fear of Islamists Drives Growth of Far Right in Belgium"
by Craig S. Smith
New York Times, February 12, 2005

ANTWERP, Belgium—Filip Dewinter, a boyish man in a dark blue suit, bounds up two flights of steep stairs in his political party's 19th-century headquarters building where posters show a Muslim minaret rising menacingly above the Gothic steeple of the city's cathedral.

"The radical Muslims are organizing themselves in Europe," he declared. "Other political parties, they are very worried about the Muslim votes and say let's be tolerant, while we are saying—the new political forces in Europe are saying—no, we should defend our identity."

From the Freedom Party in Austria to the National Front in France to the Republicans in Germany, Europe's far right has made a comeback in recent years, largely on the strength of anti-immigration feelings sharpened to a fear of Islam. That fear is fed by threats of terrorism, rising crime rates among Muslim youth and mounting cultural clashes with the Continent's growing Islamic communities.

But nowhere has the right's revival been as swift or as strong as in Belgium's Dutch-speaking region of Flanders, where support for Mr. Dewinter's Vlaams Belang, or Flemish Interest, has surged from 10 percent of the electorate in 1999 to nearly a quarter today.

Vlaams Belang is now the strongest party in Flanders, with support from a third of the voters in Antwerp, the region's largest city. Many people worry that the appeal of anti-Islamic politics will continue to spread as Europe's Muslim population grows.

"What they all have in common is that they use the issue of immigration and Islam to motivate and mobilize frustrated people," said Marco Martiniello, a political scientist at the University of Liège in the French-speaking part of Belgium. "In Flanders all attempts to counter the march of the Vlaams Belang have had no results, or limited results, and no one really knows what to do."

Fear of Islam's transforming presence is so strong that even many members of Antwerp's sizable Jewish community now support Mr. Dewinter's party, even though its founders included men who sympathized and collaborated with the Nazis during World War II.

Many of those supporters are Jews who feel threatened by a new wave of anti-Semitism emanating from Europe's growing Muslim communities. The friction is acutely felt in central Antwerp, where the Jewish quarter abuts the newer Muslim neighborhood of Borgerhout.

There, Hasidic diamond traders cross paths daily with Muslim youths, for many of whom conservative Islam has become an ideology of rebellion against perceived oppression. Israeli-Palestinian violence produces a dangerous echo here: anti-Israel marches have featured the burning in effigy of Hasidic Jews, and last June a Jewish teenager was critically wounded in a knife attack by a group of Muslim youths.

"Their values are not the right values," said Henri Rosenberg, a Talmudic scholar and lawyer who is an Orthodox Jew, speaking of the Muslim community. Though he is the son of concentration camp survivors and his grandparents died in camps, he campaigned on behalf of Vlaams Belang, then named Vlaams Blok, in regional elections last year.

As the right rallies beneath an anti-Muslim banner, European Muslims themselves have become increasingly politically engaged.

The community is far too divided along religious, racial and national lines to present a unified political force, so most of Europe's Muslim politicians have allied themselves with socialists or other left-leaning parties. But radical Muslims are also getting involved, and in many ways they are helping to validate the fears that keep parties like Vlaams Belang alive.

Behind the wooden door of a brick Brussels town house, Jean-François Bastin, 61, a Belgian convert to Islam, holds court before a steady stream of Islamic activists. His fledgling Young Muslims Party is one of the new groups aggressively pursuing pro-Muslim agendas in Europe.

He calls Osama bin Laden "a modern Robin Hood," and the World Trade Center attacks "a poetic act," "a pure abstraction." His 23-year-old son is in jail in Turkey on charges that he was involved in the bombings there that killed 61 people in November 2003.

But Mr. Bastin argues that his son's troubles are evidence that Muslim youths feel politically excluded in Europe. He says political engagement is an antidote to militancy.

"There is deviance because people don't find their place here," he said, a long, hennaed beard falling over the front of his Arab-style tunic, his graying hair tucked beneath a turban fashioned from a multicolored head scarf. "If we deny that political voice that can judge and determine what is good for Muslims, from the point of view of their religion and their citizenship, their children are going to look for adventures elsewhere."

Mr. Bastin, who converted to Islam in 1972 after a spiritual quest led him to Morocco, dismisses the far right's fears of an Islamization of Europe, even if he does dream of an Islamic theocracy governing the Continent someday.

"Were not talking about Shariah now," he said, referring to the Islamic legal code that fundamentalist Muslims believe should be the foundation of society. "Were talking about Belgian Muslims being recognized on the same footing as other confessions and ideologies."

In many ways radical Islamists like Mr. Bastin are holding Europe's broader, moderate Muslim population hostage, attracting attention disproportionate to their numbers.

"You have, in the current context, people who feel legitimized being anti-Muslim," said Mr. Martiniello, the political scientist. He cited the case of a Belgian man who had received death threats for employing a woman who wore a Muslim head scarf.

Many of the extreme right's supporters see Islam's growing European presence as the latest, most powerful surge of a

Muslim tide that has ebbed and flowed since the religion spread to the Continent in the eighth century. They warn that lax immigration policies, demographic trends and a strong Muslim agenda will forever alter Europe.

The Continent's Muslim population, now 20 million, grew from a postwar labor shortage that was filled with workers from North Africa and Turkey. By the 1980's economic malaise and rising unemployment had created tension between the largely Muslim immigrants and the surrounding societies.

But family reunion policies, which granted visas to family members of immigrants already in Europe, fueled another, more sustained wave of immigration that continues today.

"We were very naïve," Mr. Dewinter said of the liberal policies. He called tolerance Europe's Achilles' heel and immigration Islam's Trojan horse.

The trend is even more distressing to the far right when considering the low birthrate of Europe's traditional populations and the likelihood that more workers will need to be imported in the coming decades to broaden the tax bases of the Continent's aging societies.

Already about 4,000 to 5,000 Flemish residents are leaving Antwerp every year, while 5,000 to 6,000 non-European immigrants arrive annually in the city, Mr. Dewinter said. Within 10 years, he predicts, people of non-European backgrounds will account for more than a third of Antwerp's population.

"It's growing very, very fast," Mr. Dewinter said. "Maybe that will be the end of Europe."

As discussed in the previous articles, the growth of Muslim immigrant populations in Europe has not occurred without conflict. One of the most notorious examples took place in the Netherlands in November 2004. Theo van Gogh, a flamboyant filmmaker and political gadfly, was shot and stabbed to death by a young Muslim son of Moroccan immigrants after making a film denouncing the violent treatment of Muslim women. Van Gogh had also previously made a series of outrageously provocative anti-Muslim statements and gestures. In the aftermath of the killing, two members of the Dutch parliament—one of them the leader of a right-wing party with an anti-immigration platform, the other a Muslim immigrant who worked with van Gogh on his film—have been forced into hiding after receiving death threats. The New York Times *article below explains the situation.* —*JJ*

"The Hague Journal; 2 Dutch Deputies On the Run, From Jihad Death Threats"
by Marlise Simons
New York Times, March 4, 2005

Every evening, plainclothes police officers escort two members of the Dutch Parliament to armored cars and take them to hiding places for the night. One of them, Geert Wilders, has been camping out in a cell in a high-security prison where his life, he said, has become "like a bad B-movie." His colleague, Ayaan Hirsi Ali, has grown increasingly miserable sleeping on a military base.

The special treatment would certainly seem warranted: both have received a deluge of death threats since they strongly criticized the behavior of militant Muslim immigrants in the Netherlands.

After two previous political assassinations, Dutch officials are taking the threats seriously, treating the safety of the two lawmakers both as a matter of personal protection and as an issue of national security. Several politicians have said that in the country's present polarized mood, public violence could erupt if either of the two were killed.

But the two legislators themselves have disturbed the officials' plans, choosing to reveal their whereabouts to protest the conditions under which they live. Neither has had a permanent home since November, when a filmmaker, Theo van Gogh, was shot and knifed to death on an Amsterdam street. A 26-year-old Dutch-Moroccan, Muhammad Bouyeri, has been charged with the murder.

The decision by Mr. Wilders and Ms. Hirsi Ali to reveal their secret lives, one in a jail cell, the other on a naval base, has raised a question that is troubling many Dutch: is it acceptable for legislators in a Western democracy to be forced to go into hiding, to live like fugitives on the run in their own land?

"Of course this is an outrage," said Abram de Swaan, a prominent sociologist. "It's not bearable. The government must come up with better solutions, like putting them in protected homes. That's the way it happens in other countries."

The *NRC Handelsblad*, a leading daily newspaper, ran an editorial recently headlined "Unacceptable." A situation in which legislators are "hampered in carrying out their tasks puts democracy in question and makes terror successful," it said, adding that the official bureaucracy evidently "does not know how to deal with the new reality" in which Muslim terrorism may also threaten Dutch politicians.

Officials point out that the government is prosecuting several men for death threats and has adopted tough laws against terrorism suspects, including voiding their Dutch nationality. Late last month the Justice Ministry announced that it planned to expel three Muslim preachers for spreading radical Islamic ideology at a mosque in the city of Eindhoven.

Mr. Wilders's isolation becomes quickly evident on a visit to his closely guarded office in the attic of the Dutch Parliament. In his small, windowless room, far from his colleagues, he can receive visitors only if they are carefully screened and escorted at all times.

He no longer answers his own telephone, but the threats keep showing up in his e-mail, in Internet chat rooms and Web logs. Offering some samples, he switched on his office computer and a short video appeared, featuring his photograph, the sound of gunfire over Arab music and a voice that said, "He is an enemy of Islam and should be beheaded."

"The people who threaten us are walking around free and we are the captives," Mr. Wilders said. The government has told him that he will have to wait until September for a secure home. Until then, he said, he presumably has to continue his spartan life, sleeping in a cell at Camp Zeist, deprived of family and friends. The security detail schedules weekly private meetings with his wife.

Mr. Wilders, a rising right-wing politician, feels an affinity with neoconservatives in Washington and recently visited the

United States "to gather ideas." He contends that Islamic dogmas and democracy are incompatible, and has called for a five-year halt to "third world immigration," the closing of radical mosques in the Netherlands and the preventive arrest of terrorist suspects, whom he has labeled "Islamo-fascist thugs."

It was Ms. Hirsi Ali, though, who first decided to go public with her own and Mr. Wilders's hiding places, out of frustration at the government's seeming foot-dragging over finding appropriate housing. Her own proposals were regularly rejected as unsafe, she said.

Her bodyguards, she said, have deposited her on many weeknights on a naval base in Amsterdam, or hustled her off to sleep in different hotels. "They are keeping me alive, but I cannot concentrate on my work," she said. "I need a place where I have my desk, my books, my papers, a home where I can meet with people." In the past year, her handlers have twice taken her secretly to the United States.

Ms. Hirsi Ali, a Somali-born refugee who arrived in the Netherlands in 1992 and became a member of Parliament in 2003, was under police protection even before the murder of Mr. Van Gogh, with whom she had made a short television film that denounced violence against Muslim women. Some Muslims found this deeply offensive.

The Dutch government pressed Ms. Hirsi Ali to go abroad for two months after Mr. Van Gogh was killed and a letter was found on his body threatening her. When she returned to Parliament in January, she was warmly received by her colleagues. But the pressures continue.

The wife of an Islamist militant who is in police custody told a local newspaper that Ms. Hirsi Ali, a former Muslim, would be slain by Muslim women. That would make more impact than being punished by a man, the woman said. "The sisters are patient," the woman said. They will wait, "even if it takes 10 years."

Ms. Hirsi Ali concedes she is struggling with the question of how long she can continue in politics, denouncing what she regards as the excesses of Islam. In the past she has shown she is not easily cowed, but she said a deep fatigue was setting in. "I am willing to sacrifice a great deal, but I don't know if I can live like this for a lot longer." She put her inexorable quandary this way, "The real problem is, I cannot stop because that will only serve and stimulate the terrorists."

TIMELINE

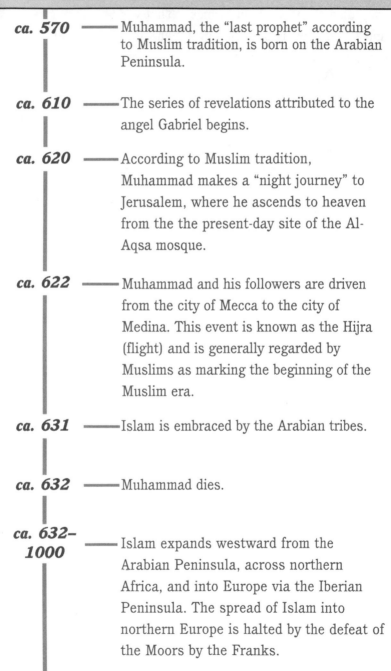

ca. 570 — Muhammad, the "last prophet" according to Muslim tradition, is born on the Arabian Peninsula.

ca. 610 — The series of revelations attributed to the angel Gabriel begins.

ca. 620 — According to Muslim tradition, Muhammad makes a "night journey" to Jerusalem, where he ascends to heaven from the the present-day site of the Al-Aqsa mosque.

ca. 622 — Muhammad and his followers are driven from the city of Mecca to the city of Medina. This event is known as the Hijra (flight) and is generally regarded by Muslims as marking the beginning of the Muslim era.

ca. 631 — Islam is embraced by the Arabian tribes.

ca. 632 — Muhammad dies.

ca. 632–1000 — Islam expands westward from the Arabian Peninsula, across northern Africa, and into Europe via the Iberian Peninsula. The spread of Islam into northern Europe is halted by the defeat of the Moors by the Franks.

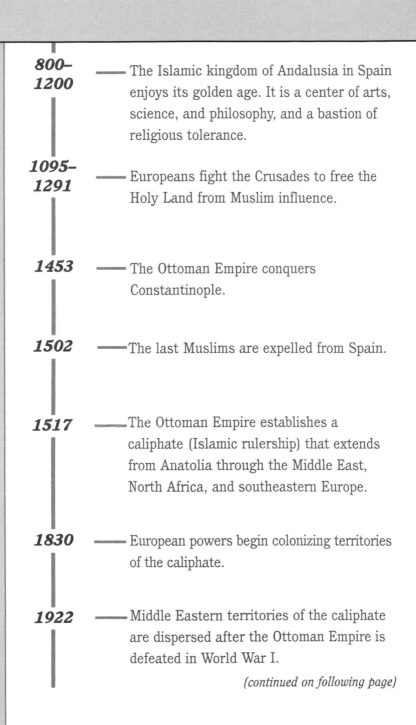

800–1200 — The Islamic kingdom of Andalusia in Spain enjoys its golden age. It is a center of arts, science, and philosophy, and a bastion of religious tolerance.

1095–1291 — Europeans fight the Crusades to free the Holy Land from Muslim influence.

1453 — The Ottoman Empire conquers Constantinople.

1502 — The last Muslims are expelled from Spain.

1517 — The Ottoman Empire establishes a caliphate (Islamic rulership) that extends from Anatolia through the Middle East, North Africa, and southeastern Europe.

1830 — European powers begin colonizing territories of the caliphate.

1922 — Middle Eastern territories of the caliphate are dispersed after the Ottoman Empire is defeated in World War I.

(continued on following page)

1947 ——The United Nations partitions Palestine into separate Jewish and Arab states; Pakistan separates from India and attains independence as an Islamic state.

1948 ——Israel declares its independence and defeats its Arab neighbors in war. Thousands of Palestinians are made refugees.

1967 ——Israel defeats Egypt, Syria, and Jordan in the Six Days' War, gaining control of the West Bank, Sinai Peninsula, Gaza Strip, and Golan Heights.

1973 ——Israel defeats Egypt, Syria, Jordan, Iraq, and forces from other Arab nations in the Yom Kippur War, securing territorial gains won in the Six Days' War.

1979 ——Islamic Revolution in Iran overthrows the shah; Ayatollah Khomeini takes power.

1979–1989 ——Backed by the United States, mujahideen (holy warriors) fight the Soviet Union in Afghanistan.

1987–1991 ——First Palestinian intifada (uprising).

1990–1991 ——First Gulf War between United States and Iraq.

1996 ——The Taliban takes power in Afghanistan.

2000 ——Second Palistinian intifada.

2001 ——Al Qaeda launches a terrorist attack on the United States.

2003 ——The second Gulf War between the United States and Iraq begins.

Middle East Institute
1761 N Street NW
Washington, DC 20036
(202) 785-1141
Web site: http://www.mideasti.org

National Council on U.S.-Arab Relations
1703 N Street NW
Suite 503
Washington, DC 20036
(202) 293-6466
Web site: http://www.ncusar.org

The United Nations
UNS-378
New York, NY 10017
(212) 963-4475
Web site: http://www.un.org

Web Sites

Due to the changing nature of Internet links, the Rosen Publishing Group, Inc., has developed an online list of Web sites related to the subject of this book. This site is updated regularly. Please use the link below to access the list:

http://www.rosenlinks.com/canf/isww

FOR FURTHER READING

Ali, Tariq. *The Clash of Fundamentalisms: Crusades, Jihads, and Money.* New York, NY: Verso, 2002.

Clark, Charles. *Islam.* San Diego, CA: Greenhaven, 2001.

Coll, Steve. *Ghost Wars: The Secret History of the CIA, Afghanistan, and Bin Laden, From the Soviet Invasion to September 10, 2001.* New York, NY: Penguin, 2001.

Dawood, N. J., trans. *The Koran.* New York, NY: Penguin, 1999.

Dudley, William, ed. *Islam* (Opposing Viewpoints). San Diego, CA: Greenhaven, 2004.

Gettleman, Marvin E., and Stuart Schaar, eds. *The Middle East and Islamic World Reader.* New York, NY: Grove Press, 2003.

Hudson, Rex A., et. al. *Who Becomes a Terrorist and Why: The 1999 Government Report on Profiling Terrorists.* Guilford, CT: The Lyons Press, 1999.

Huntington, Samuel P., et. al. *The Clash of Civilizations and the Remaking of World Order.* New York, NY: Simon and Schuster, 1996.

Laqueur, Walter, ed. *Voices of Terror: Manifestos, Writings and Manuals of Al Qaeda, Hamas, and Other Terrorists from Around the World and Throughout the Ages.* New York, NY: Reed Press, 2004.

Lewis, Bernard. *Islam and the West.* New York, NY: Oxford, 1993.

Lumbard, Joseph E. B., ed. *Islam, Fundamentalism, and the Betrayal of Tradition: Essays by Western Muslim Scholars.* Bloomington, IN: World Wisdom, 2004.

Marlin, Robert O., ed. *What Does Al-Qaeda Want? Unedited Communiques.* Berkeley, CA: North Atlantic Books, 2004.

Miller, John, and Aaron Kenedi, eds. *Inside Islam*. New York, NY: Marlowe & Company, 2002.

Milton-Edwards, Beverley, and Peter Hinchcliffe. *Conflicts in the Middle East Since 1945*. New York, NY: Routledge, 2002.

Said, Edward W. *Covering Islam: How the Media and the Experts Determine How We See the Rest of the World*. New York, NY: Random House, 1997.

Sears, Evelyn. *Muslims and the West*. Broomall, PA: Mason Crest, 2004.

ANNOTATED BIBLIOGRAPHY

Abdul-Wahhab, Shaykh Muhammad ibn. "Four Basic Rules
of Pure Monotheism." 1736. SunnahOnline.com.
Retrieved July 12, 2005 (http://www.sunnahonline.com/
ilm/aqeedah/0061.htm). Abdul-Wahhab was an eighteenth-century Muslim preacher who sought to purify
Islam of what he regarded as the corruptions that had
befallen it since the time of Muhammad. His teachings
and writings are the direct inspiration for much of the
current generation of so-called Islamic fundamentalists.
The selection here, written in 1736, represents his
teachings on Tawhid, or monotheism, a concept that is
central to Muslim belief.

Banna, Hassan al-. "Between Yesterday and Today." 1936.
Young Muslims of Maryland. Retrieved April 14, 2005
(http:// ymofmd.com/books/byat/index.htm). In this selection from an essay collection from the 1930s, the
Egyptian founder of the Muslim Brotherhood decries the
West for the materialistic, spiritually empty way of life it
has introduced to Egypt and other Muslim societies, and
proposes organized resistance.

Bin Laden, Osama, Ayman al-Zawahiri, Abu-Yasir Rifa'i Ahmad
Taha, Mir Hamzah, and Fazlur Rahman. "Jihad Against
Jews and Crusaders." In *Voices of Terror: Manifestos, Writings
and Manuals of Al Qaeda, Hamas, and Other Terrorists from
Around the World and Throughout the Ages*. Edited by Walter
Laqueur, pp.411–412. New York, NY: Reed Press, 2004.
Osama bin Laden and the leaders of four other militant
Islamic groups call on all Muslims to engage in a holy war
against the United States and its people.

Hudson, Rex, and the Staff of the Federal Research Division of the Library of Congress. *Who Becomes a Terrorist and Why: The 1999 Government Report on Profiling Terrorists*. Washington, DC: Library of Congress, 1999. A government report on profiling terrorists examines the motivations of suicide bombers.

Huntington, Samuel P. "The Clash of Civilizations?" *Foreign Affairs*, Vol. 27, No. 3, Summer 1993, pp. 22–28. Huntington, professor and foreign policy advisor, suggests that in today's world the chief conflicts will be between "cultural entities." This thesis has been as influential as it has been controversial, with obvious relevance for understanding relations between Western and Islamic societies. *Reprinted by permission of FOREIGN AFFAIRS, (Summer 1993). Copyright (1993) by the Council on Foreign Relations, Inc.*

Khomeini, Ayatollah Ruholla. *Hukumat-i-Islami* [Islamic Government]. 1970. The Virtual Vendee. Retrieved on April 14, 2005 (http://www.wandea.org.pl/iran-khomeini-pdf.htm). The Muslim holy man who inspired the Iranian Revolution of the 1970s and headed the resulting Islamic state explains the religious, moral, and social justifications for establishing Islamic governments.

Le Quesne, Nicholas. "Islam in Europe: A Changing Faith." *Time Europe*, Vol. 158, No. 26, December 24, 2001. Retrieved April 14, 2005 (http://www.time.com/time/ europe/eu/magazine/0,13716,188641,00.html). A foreign correspondent's overview of the integration of Islam into European societies. *© 2001 TIME Inc. reprinted by permission.*

Lewis, Bernard. "The Roots of Muslim Rage." *Atlantic Monthly*, Vol. 266, No. 3, September 1990, pp. 47–58. For better or worse, this article by the dean of Western scholars of the

Arab world has, since its publication, set the terms for any discussion of Islam and the Western world. The events of September 11, 2001, only made it seem more prophetic. © *Bernard Lewis, "The Roots of Muslim Rage," was first published in* The Atlantic Monthly, *vol. 266 (September 1990). A more extended version was published in book form under the title,* What Went Wrong? Western Impact and Middle Eastern Response, *Oxford University Press, New York, NY 2002.*

Maududi, Sayyid Abul Ala. *Towards Understanding Islam.* Lahore, Pakistan: Islamic Publications, 1960. Young Muslims of Maryland. Retrieved April 14, 2005 (http://www.ymofmd. com/books/tui/tui.html). Together with al-Qutb, the Pakistani Muslim Maududi is one of the most important intellectual figures of the modern Islamist movements. In this selection from one of his more than 100 books, he explains how embracing the Muslim concept of Tawhid can serve as the basis for a true and complete understanding of the entire world, in all its mystifying complexities and manifestations.

Qutb, Sayyid al-. *Milestones.* Beirut, Lebanon: Holy Koran Publishing House, 1980. Young Muslims of Maryland. Retrieved April 14, 2005 (http://www.ymofmd.com/books/ Milestone/default.htm). The Egyptian writer Sayyid al-Qutb has been called the intellectual inspiration for the modern radical Islamic movement. The selection here is from his famous introduction to his book *Milestones,* originally published in 1964, which was inspired by the time he spent in the United States in the 1940s.

Roy, Olivier. "Neo-Fundamentalism." The Social Science Research Council. Retrieved April 14, 2005 (http://www. ssrc.org/sept11/essays/roy.htm). The research director at the French National Center for Scientific Research outlines

the ways in which modern Islamist movements are transforming the contemporary geopolitical landscape.
Reprinted with permission from Olivier Roy. Mr. Roy is also the author of "Globalized Islam" by Columbia University Press, 2004.

Said, Edward. "Islam Through Western Eyes." *Nation*, Vol. 230, No. 16, April 26, 1980, pp. 488–492. The world's best-known Palestinian intellectual and champion of the rights of the Palestinian people expresses concern that in the Western world, especially in the media, the use of the term "Islam" has become a pejorative "form of attack."
"Islam Through Western Eyes (Excerpt)" by Edward Said. Reprinted with permission from the April 26, 1980 issue of The Nation. *For subscription information, call 1-800-333-8536. Portions of each week's* Nation *magazine can be accessed at http://www. thenation.com*

Simons, Marlise. "The Hague Journal; 2 Dutch Deputies On the Run, From Jihad Death Threats." *New York Times*, March 4, 2005. A reporter examines the aftermath of a political murder in the Netherlands that has its citizens wondering whether the secular values of Dutch culture are incompatible with the Islamic values of its largest immigrant group.
Copyright © 2005 by The New York Times Co. Reprinted with permission.

Smith, Craig S. "Fear of Islamists Drives Growth of Far Right in Belgium." *New York Times*, February 12, 2005. A European correspondent for the most important American newspaper examines one example of the type of conflicts arising in European societies as a result of large-scale European immigration.
Copyright © 2005 by The New York Times Co. Reprinted with permission.

Suellentrop, Chris. "Abdullah Azzam: The Godfather of Jihad." Slate.com, April 16, 2002. Retrieved April 14, 2005 (http://slate.msn.com/?id=2064385). An online journalist provides a brief overview of the life of Abdullah Azzam,

who was a founder of Hamas, financier of the mujahideen in Afghanistan, and mentor of Osama bin Laden.
Copyright 2004, Slate.com and the Washington Post. *Newsweek Interactive. All rights reserved.*

Taliban Officials. "Decrees by the Taliban." From "Afghanistan: Behind the Headlines." Moesgaard Museum Exhibition, December 1, 2001, to February 1, 2005. Retrieved July 12, 2005. (http://moesgaard. hum.au.dk/Afghanistan/ie050501.html) These Taliban decrees were featured as part of the Web material for an exhibit at the Moesgaard Museum in Arhus, Denmark. The Moesgaard gives their source for the decrees as Ahmed Rashid, a Pakistani journalist well known for his coverage of the Taliban.

Taymiyah, Taqi ad-Din Ahmad ibn. "The Religious and Moral Doctrine of Jihad." In *Voices of Terror: Manifestos, Writings and Manuals of Al Qaeda, Hamas, and Other Terrorists from Around the World and Throughout the Ages*. Edited by Walter Laqueur, pp. 391–393. New York, NY: Reed Press, 2004. An important medieval commentator on the Koran and Islamic doctrine provides an early justification for jihad that continues to influence today's Islamist groups.

Weil, Patrick. "A Nation in Diversity: France, Muslims and the Headscarf." OpenDemocracy.net, March 25, 2004. Retrieved April 14, 2005 (http://www.opendemocracy. net/debates/article.jsp?id=5&debateId=57&articleId= 1811). One of the architects of France's controversial "head scarf law" explains the legislation as an attempt both to uphold France's secular traditions and to ease the assimilation of young Muslim immigrants into French society.
Reprinted with permission from Patrick Weil.

Zakaria, Fareed. "The Politics of Rage: Why Do They Hate Us?" *Newsweek*, Vol. 138, No. 16, October 15, 2001. A top U.S. foreign policy expert attempts to explain the historical roots of the September 11 terrorist attacks on Washington, D.C., and New York City.

Excerpt from Newsweek, 10/15/2001 © 2001 Newsweek, Inc. All rights reserved. Reprinted by permission.

Zawahiri, Ayman al-. "Knights Under the Prophet's Banner." In *Voices of Terror: Manifestos, Writings and Manuals of Al Qaeda, Hamas, and Other Terrorists from Around the World and Throughout the Ages*. Edited by Walter Laqueur, pp. 426–433. New York, NY: Reed Press, 2004. Excerpts from a manuscript written by Osama bin Laden's right-hand man reveal the magnitude of the jihad against the West as conceived by Al Qaeda.

INDEX

About the Editor

Jonathan Johansen is a New York-based consultant specializing in the Arab world for multinational clients. He lived in the Middle East for many years.

Photo Credits

Cover © Reuters/CORBIS

Designer: Gene Mollica; Series Editor: Leigh Ann Cobb
Photo Researcher: Gene Mollica